EVEN

RD

a . Country

STEVEN
GERRARD

For Club and Country

PHIL THOMPSON

TEMPUS

Dedicated to Ellie Roe

Front cover image: Steven Gerrard at the press conference for the
Euro 2004 qualifier against Slovakia. © *Empics*

Back cover image: Steven Gerrard celebrates his fantastic goal against
Germany in England's 5-1 victory in Munich, 2004. © *Empics*

First published 2006

Tempus Publishing Limited
The Mill, Brimscombe Port,
Stroud, Gloucestershire, GL5 2QG
www.tempus-publishing.com

© Phil Thompson, 2006

British Library Cataloguing in Publication Data.
A catalogue record for this book is available from the British Library.

ISBN 0 7524 3793 3

Typesetting and origination by Tempus Publishing Limited
Printed in Great Britain

Contents

Acknowledgements

Special thanks to James Howarth, Holly Bennion and all at Tempus Publishing; to Helen, Louise, Graham and Linda, and also to Anne Johnson.

All images supplied by Empics.

Introduction

Liverpool were taking on European minnows FBK Kaunas, the champions of Lithuania, on a wet evening in August 2005. Kaunas were a neat and tidy team, but they had no penetration and the goal from them that would have made the match interesting looked extremely unlikely. Liverpool had won the away leg and were treating the game as a pre-season friendly. They were going through the motions and why shouldn't they? What was the point in picking up injuries in what was nothing more than a warm-up game? Liverpool's place in the final qualifying round for a Champions League spot looked assured. At half-time it was 0-0 and the game was dire.

In an attempt to make the second half more interesting, I placed a bet at the bookmakers inside Anfield that Steven Gerrard would score the first goal after the interval. My son-in-law looked sceptical. 'Gerrard's not even playing,' he scoffed as he put his money on Luis Garcia to hit the net first. Steven Gerrard, or 'Stevie G' as they have christened him at Anfield, was on the bench. If the match remained as uninspiring as it had been in the first half, I reasoned, they would have to bring him on.

I'd read in the programme notes that Gerrard was hoping to add to his goals tally that evening. He'd already scored six in the Reds' Champions League qualifiers against TNS and the away leg against Kaunas. Surely he'd had a word with Rafael Benitez to bring him on at some stage in the second period.

The opening stages of the second half were as bad as the first. Anfield had fallen into a slumber. Then, with about twenty minutes left, there was a murmur in the crowd that soon developed into rapturous applause. Steven Gerrard and Djibril Cissé were warming up on the touchline. Cissé is popular at Anfield, Steven Gerrard is idolised. It's the same kind of affection they had for the legends of the past such as Roger Hunt, Kevin Keegan, Kenny Dalglish and Ian Rush. Now that he had signed a new contract that would keep him at the club until he was eligible for a free bus pass, Anfield could relax and display its undoubted love for the local hero who they had expected to desert them in the summer.

Steven Gerrard doesn't do 'going through the motions' and instantly this became a totally different game. The impetus that Gerrard infused into his team had to be seen to be believed. A ball was knocked into Kaunas's penalty area and the alert midfielder pounced and scored a scrappy goal. Scrappy or not, it didn't matter. Their messiah had delivered and Anfield erupted. The Liverpool fans have a special affinity with Steven Gerrard. He's practically one of them on the pitch. Cissé scored a second goal before the end and everyone trooped out of Anfield happy. I collected my winnings on the way out and took my son-in-law for a pint, courtesy of Stevie G!

Phil Thompson, 2006

one

The Kid from the Bluebell

Steven Gerrard was born at Whiston Hospital, Liverpool on 30 May 1980. He was brought up on the Bluebell Housing Estate situated in Huyton in the Knowsley district of Liverpool. Huyton (pronounced 'Highton') was one of a number of new housing estates created by local government reform in the 1960s and early 1970s. Thousands of working-class Liverpool citizens found themselves shipped out to the outskirts of their home city by the slum clearance programme, to take up residence in the newly built Corporation houses. They may now have become citizens of the newly created districts with posh-sounding names like Cantril Farm, Gateacre and Knowsley, but they were still proud, dyed-in-the-wool Liverpudlians at heart.

Huyton, like most districts of Merseyside, has over the years produced many excellent footballers. Before Gerrard's arrival on the scene, the most notable was undoubtedly the tenacious midfield warrior Peter Reid, of Everton and England fame. Reid, like Gerrard, served his early football apprenticeship having a kickabout with his mates in the street, or in the nearby Britannic Park where local junior teams would play.

Apart from producing outstanding footballers, Huyton is notable for having had a Prime Minister as its local MP. Harold Wilson first became Member of Parliament for Huyton in 1950. He served the area for thirty-three years before his retirement from politics in 1983. Harold Wilson, like his present-day counterpart Tony Blair, was a confirmed football fan, although it was his boyhood heroes Huddersfield Town, not one of the Merseyside clubs, where the Yorkshire-born Wilson's football allegiances lay.

Like most Liverpool kids, Steven Gerrard was inspired to develop thoughts of one day becoming a professional footballer by watching football on the television with his family. He once said in an interview that his boyhood hero was Liverpool's Ronnie Whelan, who gave the Anfield club fantastic service as a midfield player during the 1980s and early 1990s. Although never a superstar in the Kenny Dalglish or John Barnes sense, Ronnie Whelan was an integral part of Liverpool's success in the 1980s. It is perhaps typical of Steven Gerrard that, unlike most young Liverpool fans of the time, he chose to study the midfield performances of Whelan when most kids only had eyes for the dazzling skills of the likes of Dalglish, Barnes and Beardsley. Even at this early stage of his football development, Steven Gerrard had a dream of one day emulating Ronnie Whelan in the engine room of his beloved Reds, winning the tackles, setting up the chances and scoring the vital goals for the Anfield giants. 'I often watched Ronnie Whelan play. He was the unsung hero in the Liverpool midfield,' said Gerrard. 'I admired the way he went about things. He made the game look easy. Every successful team needs a player like Ronnie Whelan in midfield.'

Although he was rather small for his age, Steven Gerrard impressed most onlookers right from the start of his junior football career. He played for his school team, St Michael's Primary School in Huyton, and also for Whiston Juniors. Mike Tilling was a teacher at St Michael's when Gerrard represented the school as a ten year old. Mr Tilling told the *Liverpool Echo's* Tony Barnett that young Gerrard looked a certain star of the future: 'I just couldn't believe he was so good because he was one of the smallest boys in the class. I started him off as a striker and it seemed as if he had been playing for years. He was amazing.'

Playing for Whiston Juniors it was the same story – Steven Gerrard was a sensation. Assistant coach at Whiston, Peter Leonard, recalled, 'There were seasons when he scored 100 goals – he was absolutely brilliant. I'm an Evertonian, but I keep telling everyone that we haven't seen the best of Steven Gerrard yet.'

It was inevitable that Gerrard's blossoming talent would come to the attention of one of Merseyside's professional clubs and from the age of nine he began to train at Liverpool Football Club. Jim Aspinall, chief youth scout at Liverpool's academy, was a spectator at one of Steven Gerrard's school games and was immediately impressed by the ten year old's ability. Aspinall recalled, 'He covered every blade of grass; he was magnificent. I spoke to his dad after the game and he told me that Steven had already been invited to the Liverpool Centre of Excellence by Dave Shannon, one of our coaches. I told him that was okay so long as he was coming.' Other teams that Gerrard played for as a youth were Liverpool side Denton and the Wirral's Heygarth.

If Ronnie Whelan was Steven Gerrard's biggest influence when it came to studying the skills and crafts needed to become a top footballer, his father Paul has undoubtedly been the biggest influence on his overall career. The great Bill Shankly once said, 'It is mothers and fathers who produce footballers, not coaches.' Although Gerrard was obviously given a fantastic start in his football apprenticeship by the staff at the Liverpool youth academy, he always cites his father Paul as the biggest influence on his career. In later years, when Gerrard needed help and advice on whether to remain at Anfield or join the Abramovich revolution at Chelsea, it was to his father and the rest of his family that he turned to. One thing is it extremely unlikely you will see, however, is Gerrard's father doing a Ted Beckham and writing a book about his son.

Back in the early 1990s the question of whether to go or stay was the furthest thing from the young Steven Gerrard's mind as he sat with his family watching his England heroes competing in the 1990 World Cup finals in Italy. Gerrard recalled, 'I remember sitting at home with my mum and dad and my brother when Italia '90 was on the telly. I was leaping around the house when the penalties were on. I thought about how it would be great to have been a part of that. How great it would be to make the kind of impact Paul Gascoigne did then.'

Steven Gerrard got over the disappointment of England being knocked out of the World Cup on penalties by continuing to hone his skills as a schoolboy footballer. At his secondary school, Cardinal Heenan RC High School in West Derby, Gerrard impressed his new sports teachers from the start. Eric Chadwick, P.E. teacher at the school, recalls, 'He was very slim and small, totally different to how he is today. Steven's skill came in his speed of thought and the fact that he was a yard quicker than every other boy. He was naturally gifted and brilliant at any sport. I remember him playing for the school in a Royal Mail Trophy final. He was amazing and won the game for us.'

Mr Chadwick remembered that the young Steven was so obsessed with the game that he would even go on scouting missions to check out future opponents, 'One Saturday morning Steve went with his dad to watch Cardinal Heenan's next opponents in a cup match. On Monday, Steve knocked on my office door to give me a detailed report on the team we were due to play. I knew then that this thirteen year old had something more than any of our other football-daft youngsters.'

Steven Gerrard's lack of inches was a cause of concern for his football coaches during his early teenage years. It was obvious for all to see that he possessed outstanding football ability, but he began to develop niggling injury problems. His Cardinal Heenan coach, Eric Chadwick, told the *Liverpool Echo* that Gerrard failed to gain selection for the England Schoolboys team because of muscular injuries: 'Steven was having all kinds of problems with injuries. Basically his muscles were outgrowing his bones and it meant he kept getting all kinds of strains and pulls.' Although obviously disappointed to miss out on an invitation to join the National Centre of Excellence at Lilleshall, the young football prodigy got his head down and continued to display his awesome talent for his school and the Liverpool Schoolboys team.

At the age of sixteen Steven Gerrard was invited by Liverpool FC to join their Youth Academy. There then followed an amazing transformation in the size and physique of the Liverpool youngster that transformed the Bambi-like teenager into a strapping young man. Tim Johnson was Gerrard's coach for the Liverpool Schoolboys team and couldn't believe the change in him. He recalled, 'Young Stevie had the most amazing growth spurt. I was at the Liverpool Academy one day – this was eighteen months after Steven had finished playing for me. When I saw him I couldn't believe it; the Bambi that had left me had changed into a bison. When I first met him as a thirteen year old he was a very quiet lad with these legs which went all the way up to his neck. I just couldn't believe the change in him. I couldn't take it in that it was the same Steven Gerrard.'

With the scrawny youngster now metamorphosised into a strapping sixteen year old, the time was now right for Steve Heighway and his youth academy team at Liverpool, which consisted of Frank Skelly, Dave Shannon and Hughie McAuley, to turn the incredibly gifted Gerrard into an outstanding footballer.

Steven Gerrard was now a YTS trainee at Anfield, along with future Liverpool stars David Thompson, Michael Owen and Jamie Carragher. Thompson, Owen and Carragher were older than Gerrard and were key members of the Liverpool Youth team that won the FA Youth Challenge Cup in 1996. Steven Gerrard did make several appearances in the cup run, but did not appear in the team that beat West Ham in the final. Liverpool, with goals from Newby and Larmour in the first leg and Owen and Quinn in the second, beat West Ham 4-1 on aggregate to take the trophy. At this stage all the talk at Anfield, when it came to up-and-coming talent, was about a kid named Michael Owen who might just be another Ian Rush.

two

Young, Gifted and Red

During the 1996/97 season Steven Gerrard was hoping to establish himself in the Under-17s academy team at Anfield and perhaps even make a reserve team appearance. He was still only sixteen years old when disaster struck. A serious foot injury severely curtailed his Liverpool ambitions and he was on the injured list for almost twelve months. When Gerrard recovered from this period of inactivity and regained his fitness he really began to make the academy staff at Anfield sit up and take notice.

Season 1997/98 will always be remembered for Michael Owen's explosion onto the international stage. Owen's incredible goal against Argentina at France '98 will be talked about for as long as the game is played. Sitting at home in Huyton, watching his former Liverpool Youth team colleague take the world of football by storm, was Steven Gerrard. Now fully recovered from the injury that had put his career temporarily on hold, he was confident that one day he would also take part in the world's greatest football tournament.

When the 1998/99 season began at Anfield hopes were high that the newly installed joint team manager, Gerard

Houllier, would form a successful partnership with Roy Evans. Evans had been at Anfield, as a player and then a coach, since the Shankly era of the 1960s. Gerard Houllier had been a Liverpool fan since he had stood on the Kop on a cold September evening in 1969 and watched Shankly's team demolish Dundalk 10-0 in a European Fairs Cup game. 'I am a real Liverpool supporter,' stated Houllier. 'I am here because Roy Evans wanted me to come to Anfield and I agreed on the condition that he stayed on and we worked together.' The Liverpool fans liked what they heard. Liverpool's executive vice-chairman, Peter Robinson, who was also a veteran from the Shankly days, was the person who had enticed Houllier to Liverpool. Robinson told the press, 'Gerard will bring to us coaching experience of the highest quality at both club and country level. He also possesses an unrivalled knowledge of technical excellence and innovation which has made him one of the most respected coaches in the world.'

Houllier had played a key role in bringing World Cup success to France at the 1998 tournament. Much of this success was due to the academy system which provided many of the French World Cup-winning squad. Houllier hoped that he could emulate at Anfield the academy that had proved so successful in his native country. With this in mind, talented youngsters at Anfield knew that if they proved themselves at academy and reserve team levels, then an opportunity to stake a claim for a first-team place was theirs for the taking. Steven Gerrard was fully aware of this and set about impressing Evans and Houllier as soon as the new season kicked off.

One person who had no doubts at all that Steven Gerrard would make a big impact at Anfield during the coming season was England's new goalscoring sensation Michael Owen. Apart from the staff at the Liverpool academy and others in the know at Anfield, Gerrard was virtually unknown to the rest of Merseyside and the football world in general. However, when football's new boy wonder, Michael Owen, informed *Liverpool Echo* readers that there was another kid at Anfield who was destined for England glory, football fans across Merseyside had to sit up and take notice. For most of them it was the first time they had even heard the name Steven Gerrard. With supreme optimism, Owen told *Echo* readers, 'Steve will be our star man next year. I'm not just saying this, but he is absolutely brilliant. He has got everything it takes to become a top player. He's big, strong, got speed, a good tackler and he knows a lot about the game. If I was a betting man I'd certainly put money on him becoming a full England international.' Michael Owen's prophetic words were to be borne out by events during a momentous 1998/99 season for Gerrard.

After impressing in Liverpool's early-season Under-19 youth academy games, Steven Gerrard was selected for the England Under-18 international team to play against Italy. Also selected was Gerrard's academy teammate, Stephen Wright. Steve Heishway, the director of Liverpool's youth academy accompanied the five Liverpool youths to Italy to watch the game. Both Wright and Gerrard had excellent matches in the 4-2 victory, Gerrard scoring England's fourth goal.

Frank Skelly, who works with Heighway at the academy, said that Gerrard was progressing nicely as a midfield player: 'Steven had a good all-round game. He has improved at every level as he has gone along at the academy. He sometimes needs to control his aggression, but he is a very promising midfield player.' As Frank Skelly noted, Steven Gerrard, like Michael Owen in his early days in the Liverpool academy team, was prone to the occasional flare-up. Like Owen, Gerrard began to control this side to his game as he matured as a player.

With the season barely a few months old, Steven Gerrard began to be selected for the Liverpool reserve team and did not look out of place. Gerrard had a particularly good game playing against a strong Manchester United reserve team at Old Trafford in October 1998. Reserve team coach Joe Corrigan was impressed by the youngsters who were given their chance against United. He said, 'We were very pleased with the two young lads who came on in the second half, Steven Gerrard and Alan Navarro. Both have come through the Academy League into the reserve team and did really well.'

A few weeks later Steven Gerrard received his marching orders while playing against Everton in an Under-19s academy game for an 'uncompromising tackle'. Gerrard was then Liverpool's star performer for the reserves against Leeds United in a fixture that took place in November. The staff at Anfield now knew that the time was right to blood the Huyton youngster in the first team.

When the Liverpool squad travelled to Spain to take on Celta Vigo in the 24 November fixture in the UEFA Cup, Steven Gerrard, along with Stephen Wright, was selected to travel with the party. Wright actually made his first-team debut, coming on in the second half of the 3-1 defeat. Gerrard had to wait until the following Sunday's Premiership fixture against Blackburn Rovers to make his Liverpool debut. The date was 29 November 1998 and he came on for Vegard Heggem in the final minutes of the 2-0 home victory against the Lancashire side. Steven Gerrard's first full game for Liverpool at Anfield was against Celta Vigo in the return leg of their UEFA Cup tie. Gerrard had waited all his life for this moment, since he had first kicked a ball around the streets and parks of Huyton, and now it had arrived.

When Steven Gerrard ran out at Anfield on 8 December 1998 it began a chain of events that would lead to the midfielder emerging as the most popular player among the supporters since the heyday of Kenny Dalglish. Liverpool needed to defeat the Spanish side by two clear goals to stand any chance of progressing. Obviously nervous on the day of the match after he was informed at one o'clock that he would start the game, he phoned his friends and family to tell them the news that he was to make his home debut that evening. Before kick-off he was given a brief pep talk by Gerard Houllier and his new assistant Phil Thompson. Roy Evans had decided to call it a day a few weeks prior to the Celta Vigo games after realising that his role as joint Liverpool manager was not working out. The nervous youngster was basically told by Houllier and Thompson to go out and enjoy the occasion. It took Gerrard a little while to settle down but once he touched the ball a few times the pre-match nerves went away.

Liverpool lost the game 1-0 to a decent Spanish outfit who looked as if they would go far in the competition. Although he was disappointed to have made a losing start on his Anfield debut, Gerrard was pleased to find out after the game that he had been named the Carlsberg Man of the Match. He had shown the Anfield faithful and the Liverpool management that the big occasion did not faze him in the slightest.

Liverpool's England star Paul Ince, the midfielder that Gerrard would ultimately replace in the Reds' line-up, was impressed by Gerrard's first few games in the Liverpool first team. He told the press, 'It was good to see young Steven Gerrard making his Liverpool debut when he played the first hour at Spurs a few days before the Celta Vigo game. He showed some nice little touches and he's definitely one for the future. White Hart Lane is not an easy place to play for your first game, but he did well.'

Steven Gerrard, in fact, could quite easily have been playing for Spurs against Liverpool on that December afternoon in 1998. Gerrard made his Under-17s Liverpool academy debut against the London side a couple of years prior to the 1998 fixture. The Spurs chairman Alan Sugar was so impressed with the Liverpool youngster that after the game he offered the Anfield club £2.5 million to take him to White Hart Lane there and then. The Liverpool staff were slightly taken aback, but lost little time in declining Sugar's sensational offer.

After some impressive displays, Steven Gerrard was now a member of the Liverpool first-team squad and trained with the club's top players at Melwood instead of at the academy. These were heady times for the Huyton teenager and he was determined to make the most of his opportunity. 'The manager has given me my chance and I'm really pleased that it has come so early,' remarked a delighted Gerrard. 'I can't pretend I expected to be in the first-team squad so soon, but I think the manager has been pleased with me. I don't think I looked out of place in the first team. I have always dreamt of playing at Anfield. The great thing about Liverpool is that they might have millions to spend, but they do give youngsters a chance.'

It was during the pre-Christmas period of 1998 that Steven Gerrard picked up a medal as a member of the Liverpool team that defeated Burscough 2-1 in the Liverpool Senior Cup final. The team comprised youth academy and reserve-team players. In goal for Liverpool that evening was Tony Warner, who is now making a name for himself at Fulham. Gareth Roberts, Richie Partridge and Alan Navarro were also in the Liverpool side that won the trophy and all have gone on to make careers for themselves in professional football. Alan Navarro scored a fabulous goal for Liverpool to win the game and was expected to develop into an outstanding midfield player for the Reds. Interviewed in April 2000, the eighteen year old was still waiting for his Liverpool first-team breakthrough, but said that Steven Gerrard's success was an inspiration to all the young players at Anfield: 'Steven is an example to us all that if you are good enough then your chance will come along. He has done really well for himself and deservedly so, because he is a top-class player.' Alan Navarro eventually left Liverpool to try his luck across the Mersey at Tranmere Rovers.

With Jamie Redknapp and Paul Ince established England internationals, it was never going to be easy for Steven Gerrard to carve out a permanent midfield place for himself in the first team at Anfield. As the 1998/99 season reached its conclusion, Gerrard was happy to be selected in any position that Liverpool wanted him to fill. 'My aim between now and the end of the season is to play as many games as possible and to carry on improving and to steer clear of injuries,' he told the local press in March 1999.

On the pitch the 1998/99 season was turning out to be a disaster for Liverpool. Celta Vigo had dumped them out of the UEFA Cup before Christmas and Spurs had progressed at their expense in the League Cup. In the FA Cup Manchester United had knocked the Reds out in the fourth round, so there was only respectability in the Premiership to aim for. Some football pundits were calling Houllier's team the worst seen at Anfield since before Bill Shankly took over the club in 1959. Steven Gerrard may have been on a high, but his team looked to be in dire straits. The Reds were performing so badly in the Premiership that there was even talk of them considering the option of attempting to gain entry to the following season's UEFA Cup through the Intertoto Cup route! Liverpool's proud reputation as one of Europe's finest looked to be in tatters.

To add to Houllier's misery, local hero Steve McManaman was set to leave for Real Madrid as soon as the season ended. There was also the fact that McManaman's England team-mate Paul Ince now only occasionally showed glimpses of the outstanding ability that had once made him one of the Premiership's most outstanding midfield stars.

Obviously Houllier would need time to get things right at Anfield. Ince might have been struggling to recapture his best form as Liverpool attempted to end the season on a positive note, but he still found time to express his delight at Gerrard's invitation to join up with the full England squad for training. Ince told the press, 'I was really pleased that young Steven Gerrard has been called up by Kevin Keegan to train with the England squad. I played alongside Steven for the reserves at Nottingham Forest the other day and he was fantastic. He looked to have everything you need to be a very good midfield player. The more games he plays for Liverpool the better he will become.'

Gerrard's England invitation took him completely by surprise. He had had an outstanding game for Liverpool in their 3-2 defeat against Derby County early in March, but to get invited to train with Keegan's first England squad after becoming the new national manager came out of the blue.

Steven Gerrard travelled to Bisham Abbey with his Anfield teammates Michael Owen, Jamie Redknapp, Robbie Fowler and Steve McManaman. Gerrard's father, Paul, the man that the Liverpool star constantly names as the biggest influence on his career, was delighted, as were the rest of the Gerrard family back home in Huyton. Paul Gerrard told his son that this was a great opportunity and to spend as much time as possible studying the England regulars to try and glean as much as he could from watching some of the nation's top players in training.

Gerrard was welcomed on his arrival at Bisham Abbey by Kevin Keegan and Howard Wilkinson, who knew the young midfielder from the England Under-18 side. Wilkinson told Gerrard to keep on doing the things that he did for Liverpool and he would be fine. At times Gerrard's nerves got the better of him as he mixed with England's finest for the first time.

Eventually, Steven Gerrard began to settle down and show what he was capable of as he took part in the daily training sessions. Then the injury bug that had dogged Gerrard's career throughout his teenage years struck again. He felt sharp pains at the base of his back while taking a shower. He was immediately taken for an X-ray, which revealed a stress fracture to his back. It was estimated that Steven Gerrard had already lost nearly two years of his career through injuries and the thought of another long spell on the sidelines filled him with despair. Kevin Keegan gave the distressed youngster a confidence-boosting pep talk before dispatching Gerrard back to Anfield for further medical examinations. A scan revealed that the stress fracture had been there since Gerrard was born and the medical advice was that although he had to cut down on weight training he was free to train as normal for the rest of the season. Steven Gerrard breathed a mighty sigh of relief before joining up with his Anfield teammates as they attempted to salvage something from a poor season.

Michael Owen was another Liverpool youngster who suffered with injury throughout the final stages of the 1998/99 season and after playing against Leeds early in April he missed the final stages of the campaign with hamstring and tendon damage. This put Owen out for three months. The Liverpool goalscoring sensation was paying the price for almost three seasons of non-stop football. Owen had suffered three hamstring injuries since his 1998 World Cup exploits and it was hoped that a long summer rest would cure the problem. The injury put Owen out of England's vital European Championship qualifiers against Sweden and Bulgaria due to take place in June. Steven Gerrard's season came to an end at practically the same time as Owen's and after the Leeds game he took part in just two more Liverpool games. Niggling injuries meant that Gerrard's momentous first season in the Liverpool first team finished on an unsatisfactory note.

Despite these end-of-season setbacks, Steven Gerrard was now firmly established at the club. He had started the campaign hoping to play as many academy and reserve-team games as possible. At the end of it he had won England Under-18 cups and had even trained with the national side. He was also a first-team player for his club and was being described by many pundits as the greatest midfield prospect in British football.

Michael Owen was delighted that his friend had made such giant steps during the season. Owen remarked, 'Steven has made his full Liverpool debut and he has come through the ranks with me. It was great to see him get the first-team chance after having to wait for a while. I know he is going to be a star of the future.'

As for Liverpool's first season with Houllier in charge, Owen said, 'Gerard has not made any drastic changes since taking over from Roy Evans. He has brought in new staff to deal with fitness and things like that. Hopefully he will continue to make us a better team. We want to win the League next season.'

three

The Brightest Star

As expected, Liverpool finished 1998/99 out of the UEFA Cup places, but decided against competing in the Intertoto Cup. Alex Ferguson's outstanding Manchester United team won their fifth Premiership title in seven seasons. Liverpool did, however, win three pieces of silverware during a disappointing campaign. In pre-season tournaments they had picked up the Pirelli Cup and the Carlsberg Trophy, and to add to these triumphs they beat Sunderland at the end of the 1998/99 season to collect the Football League Centenary Challenge Cup. Gerard Houllier had an almighty task on his hands in his attempt to win some meaningful trophies for the Reds, but with young players of the calibre of Owen, Thompson, Carragher and Gerrard now at his disposal, the future did look bright.

Another academy youngster, Stephen Wright, was also expected to make a first-team breakthrough in the coming season. Wright's Liverpool career had almost run parallel with Gerrard's. 'We grew up with each other,' recalled Wright. 'We'd been playing against each other for years and then we both went to Liverpool. I'm made up to see the gaffer give Stevie Gerrard a chance because it gives me a boost to see young players getting a chance. When Stevie gets his injuries sorted out he'll be top class.' Wright hoped that his Premiership debut would not be in the too distant future.

With Manchester United having defeated Bayern Munich in the 1999 European Cup final to add to their Premiership and FA Cup trophies, Liverpool began the 1999/2000 season knowing that they had fallen a long way behind their deadly North West rivals. Houllier had made some exciting summer signings, bringing Sami Hyypia, Dietmar Hamann, Vladimir Smicer, Stephane Henchoz and Sander Westerveld to Anfield. There had been rumours for a while that Robbie Fowler would follow his great friend Steve McManaman and leave Liverpool for pastures new. He was linked with a £12 million move to Arsenal or Manchester United but when the new season began he was still playing in the red of Liverpool rather than the red and white of their two Premiership rivals.

Michael Owen had still not recovered from his hamstring injury at the start of the campaign, but Steven Gerrard was fit and ready for the new season to begin. With Paul Ince, Steve McManaman and Oyvind Leonhardsen among the Anfield players to have left the club before the start of the new season, the opportunity for Gerrard to cement his place in the Liverpool line-up was there for the taking.

The season would also prove to be a crucial one for other lads, like David Thompson and Danny Murphy. Jamie Carragher was by now a permanent fixture in the team and would remain so for years to come. With Robbie Fowler pledging his future to the club, for the first time in many years Liverpool was a team packed with local talent. Michael Owen knew that this was a crucial season for the Reds. He remarked, 'Critics are saying Liverpool are not feared any more. We have to regain the respect we once held in the world and it's no good our just talking about it. We have to do it on the pitch. Last season we did well against the better teams, but we have been inconsistent against lesser sides.'

Robbie Fowler was delighted that his future had been settled and told the press that he was determined to win silverware at Liverpool: 'I signed a new contract with Liverpool because I want to help Liverpool get back to winning trophies. That is my only concern.' Fowler would have to wait another season to fulfil his wish when the Reds would once again hit the trophy trail.

Gerard Houllier's assistant Phil Thompson echoed Michael Owen's comments when he said that Liverpool needed to be more consistent against the lesser teams. Thompson said, 'I don't want to be like other teams, raising their game for one-offs. I want Liverpool to be more consistent. We play a lot more "lesser" teams in the Premiership than we do top ones, so if you beat more "lesser" teams you will gain more points.'

Steven Gerrard was determined that the new season would be one in which Liverpool would get closer to Manchester United. Gerrard remarked, 'United have set the standards over the past few seasons, but we know that on our day we can beat anyone. Manchester United have taken the mantle that Liverpool had in the 1980s when we were the dominant team. They are a good side who have proven themselves in Europe. They deserve full credit for that.'

Gerrard missed the first game of the season away to Sheffield Wednesday. The Liverpool youngster was not even on the subs' bench for the Reds' 2-1 victory. Gerard Houllier had new £8 million signing Dietmar Hamann taking the place of Paul Ince in midfield, alongside Redknapp, Smicer and Berger in the middle of the park. Steven Gerrard knew that he had a fight on his hands to force his way into the Reds' first team at the start of the campaign. Danny Murphy, who had looked outstanding in Liverpool's pre-season friendlies, and David Thompson were also waiting in the wings for their opportunity to impress Houllier.

Steven Gerrard's chance to make his first appearance of the season came sooner than expected when it was revealed that Hamann, who had been forced to leave the field against Wednesday after a heavy challenge from Gerald Sibon, had sustained ankle ligament damage that would keep him out for at least three months. Steven Gerrard was not slow in staking his claim for Hamann's defensive midfield role and he told the *Liverpool Echo* he was raring to go. 'I've read that Didi could be out for some time and hopefully I'll get the chance on Saturday to prove what I'm made of,' said the confident Gerrard. 'I've got a bit of experience from last season and also the confidence. The boss has told me that because of injuries, suspension and lack of form Didi might not have been in for every game. I've got to be ready to step in when necessary. If Gerard Houllier gives me the go ahead to play on Saturday I'll try and make my place permanent. I want to play as many games as I can this season.'

Steven Gerrard was selected for Liverpool's first home game of the season but was substituted during a disappointing 1-0 defeat against Watford. Gerrard's ability to play in a number of positions meant that he was never likely to have been out of the first-team frame for long. The Liverpool teenager's confidence in advertising himself for first-team selection, however, echoed the time when another Liverpool youth in the early 1960s did exactly the same thing with the legendary Bill Shankly. Legend has it that Tommy Smith injured one of Shankly's first-team regulars during a Melwood training session with a ferocious tackle. It was then claimed that Smith knocked on Shankly's door to ask would he be taking the place of the injured first-teamer for Saturday's fixture!

It is clear for all to see that Steven Gerrard is similar to Tommy Smith in many ways. He is a local lad that the Anfield faithful have taken to in a big way. He can play in a variety of positions and is equally as good in all of them.

28

Gerrard also possesses fierce tackling ability and is capable of scoring crucial goals, just like Tommy Smith did for his beloved Liverpool. Contrary to the legend that has now grown around Smith, he did not get into trouble with referees as often as people think. He may have been a fierce competitor, but he knew when to keep out of trouble. Apart from his developing years in the game, Steven Gerrard also very rarely gets involved in controversy on the field of play. He gives and takes a hard challenge, but then gets on with the game in the same way that Smith usually did. Like Tommy Smith, Steven Gerrard would need every bit of self-confidence and self-belief if he was going to become a permanent fixture in the first team at Anfield but, at the time of writing, apart from the odd injury and temporary dip in form, Steven Gerrard has been a Liverpool regular since the second game of the 1999/2000 season.

One of the seasoned professionals that Gerrard was replacing in the Liverpool squad was England international Paul Ince. Ince had always encouraged up-and-coming youngsters at Anfield like Steven Gerrard and was pleased for him to be given a first-team opportunity, but Ince's departure from Anfield, when Gerard Houllier decided that he no longer figured in his reconstruction plans, was acrimonious in the extreme. According to newspaper reports Ince wanted a £1 million-plus pay-off from Liverpool. He still had five years left on his contract and was determined to make Liverpool pay up if they wanted to dump him. Houllier was determined to be seen as a manager who was totally in control of everything that took place at Anfield when it came to who he wanted in his squad and who he didn't.

Eventually Paul Ince signed for Middlesbrough and his financial differences with the club were settled. Gerard Houllier had always been regarded as a nice man who had a touch of steel about him. Anfield insiders claimed that you crossed swords with Houllier at your peril. His handling of the Paul Ince saga and the departure of other players and backroom staff during his tenure as Liverpool manager are clear examples of the fact that when Houllier made a decision there was to be no going back on it.

Steven Gerrard retained his place in the Liverpool side for their second away game of the new season at Middlesbrough, but Michael Owen was still on the injured list. Gerard Houllier was so concerned that Owen had still not recovered from his hamstring problems that he fell out with the physiotherapist who had worked tirelessly with the young striker throughout the summer months. Houllier's decision to replace Mark Leather with a new Liverpool physio was yet another example of the fact that he was not afraid to make difficult decisions if he felt they were warranted. He wanted Michael Owen ready for the new season and when he wasn't, someone had to pay. Houllier even ignored the advice of Mark Leather and sent Owen to Germany for treatment in an attempt to clear up the injury. Michael Owen did eventually make his return to first-team action at the end of August, but by that time Liverpool had lost two of their first four games, including a 1-0 loss to a Paul Ince-inspired Middlesbrough.

Despite Liverpool's poor start to the season, Steven Gerrard had been in outstanding form for the Reds in their early games. Against Middlesbrough Gerrard had not looked overawed at the prospect of pitting his skills against the might of Paul Ince in the battle for midfield supremacy. Gerrard also put in another outstanding display in Liverpool's 2-1 victory over Leeds a few days later. The young midfielder was rewarded for his impressive early-season form with a call-up to the England Under-21 squad. Many soccer pundits were now predicting that Steven Gerrard was a certainty to win a full England cap at some stage in the near future.

Liverpool's most impressive performance of the season came when Arsenal visited Anfield at the end of August.

Goals from Robbie Fowler and Patrick Berger gave the Reds an excellent 2-0 victory. Fowler's goal was a thirty-yard stunner and was an early contender for goal of the season. To add to Liverpool's glee, Michael Owen made his first appearance of the season, coming on near the end of the match to send the Anfield crowd into raptures. Although Robbie Fowler was the Liverpool Man of the Match, Steven Gerrard was not far behind him with another impressive display. Gerrard was now filling the role that Didi Hamann had been signed to play with growing assurance. Showing a remarkable maturity for his years, Gerrard played a role which saw him winning the midfield battles with crisp tackles before spraying out inch-perfect passes to the attacking members of the team. It would have been easy for him to stray into attacking positions himself, but this would have left the Liverpool defence exposed. Gerard Houllier had told him exactly how he wanted him to play and this was the role Steven Gerrard carried out to perfection.

In the Arsenal game Steven Gerrard was up against one of the great midfield players in European football in Patrick Vieira. Gerrard did not look the least bit overawed. The Liverpool youngster even seemed at home answering questions from the press after the game, saying that he was delighted to see his friend Michael Owen back in the squad again. Gerrard said, 'You heard the fans when Michael came on. They love him here and it's great to have him back. Having Michael available again will give the manager a headache, as will having Didi Hamann and Vladimir Smicer back when they are fit again.'

Gerard Houllier was as delighted as his team were after their great performances against Arsenal and Leeds and he remarked, 'Last season we couldn't beat any of the top four teams. Arsenal and Leeds were two of those top four clubs. I still think Arsenal are a better team than us, but we are improving.'

Gerard Houllier was delighted with the improvement in Liverpool's form, but he was still on the lookout for players who would improve his squad. He came close to signing top French defender Mikael Silvestre but Alex Ferguson got there before him and took the young France Under-21 international to Old Trafford.

Young local talent at Anfield, however, such as David Thompson, Jamie Carragher and Steven Gerrard, were determined to impress on Gerard Houllier that kids from Merseyside could save the club a lot of money. David Thompson was keen to stress that a Liverpool team sprinkled with talented academy graduates could pay dividends for the Reds: 'We have got a lot of local lads in our team and I know from the fans' point of view how important that is. Jamie Carragher has been in the team for a couple of seasons now, while Steven Gerrard has only recently come onto the scene, but he has done really well. I think myself and Steve bring aggression and enthusiasm to the midfield. Having this type of aggression and enthusiasm is important and I know that Steven is hoping, like I do, that when the other lads are fit we can still keep our places in the team.'

With Owen, Gerrard, Carragher, Fowler, Murphy and Thompson all regular Liverpool first-teamers during this period, the Reds had more local lads in their line-up than any other Premiership club. Steven Gerrard was improving with every game and one writer to the *Liverpool Echo* was certain that the young midfield dynamo was a future Anfield great. Writing in September 1999, the correspondent remarked: 'I think Liverpool have finally found the "hard" midfield man, the real ball winner we thought we had in Paul Ince. It is of course Steven Gerrard. From the first time I saw him against Celta Vigo (Dec 1998) I thought this guy has talent. His tackling is incredible and he seems to run miles and miles on the pitch. He is a class act. That is good news for Liverpool, but not so much good news for

Didi Hamann who will have to be something really special to dethrone Steven Gerrard. He will make it into the full England squad sooner than people think.'

Liverpool's good run of form suffered a setback when Manchester United came to Anfield and ran out 3-2 winners. It was from a Steven Gerrard foul on David Beckham, just outside the penalty area, that Beckham shot United into a 3-1 lead. For once Gerrard's inexperience showed, giving away a free-kick to United in such a dangerous area, but against such an outstanding team, as Ferguson's boys were at this moment in time, Liverpool had acquitted themselves well and were unlucky not to get a point. Outstanding for Manchester United in this game was the defender that Gerard Houllier had come close to signing just a few weeks earlier, Mikael Silvestre.

The performances of Liverpool's defence were gradually becoming a cause for concern to Gerard Houllier and the manner in which they allowed ten-man Leicester to snatch a draw against the Reds infuriated him further. 'I've always said that as long as we don't have clinical, rock-solid defensive play – and by that I mean the whole team working hard to protect the goal – we will never achieve anything,' remarked Houllier. 'If things don't start to work properly then other players will come in to make sure it does. At the moment only Sami Hyypia is playing consistently well in defence. I will act.' Houllier's frustration was obvious as Liverpool's defensive frailties continued to undermine everything he was attempting to achieve at Anfield.

The mood of the Liverpool boss grew even darker when Everton came to Anfield and ran out 1-0 winners in a bad-tempered Merseyside derby. Michael Owen was lucky to escape with a yellow card after a wild two-footed tackle on David Weir. In the second half, Liverpool goalkeeper Sander Westerveld and Everton's Francis Jeffers were sent off after a punch-up. This was followed by Steven Gerrard, who had come on as a late substitute, receiving a red card for a high tackle on Kevin Campbell. Everton's Don Hutchison was also lucky to escape with a lecture after some meaty challenges in a violent encounter.

Apart from losing the three points, Liverpool's dismay was further compounded by the knowledge that goal-keeper Sander Westerveld and Steven Gerrard would now receive instant three-match suspensions. An infuriated Gerard Houllier said after the game, 'I want my players to have passion and show that they want to win, but I was a bit ashamed after Monday's game because some of them took things too far.'

Anfield old boy Don Hutchison said that he did feel sympathy for the red-carded players. 'Franny Jeffers and Westerveld did lose their heads a little and Steven Gerrard had only been on the pitch for twenty minutes,' he reflected. 'Tackles like Steven Gerrard's on Kevin Campbell are what derbies are all about. Take the tackles away and it wouldn't be half as good a game.'

Steven Gerrard's dismissal may have been reckless, but he had shown this side to his game in the past. Michael Owen was also still capable of losing his head in the heat of battle and dishing out a clumsy tackle. Both Owen and Gerrard would learn from these mistakes as they gained more experience as seasoned professionals at Anfield.

For the time being, Steven Gerrard's enforced absence from the team gave him time to reflect on just what he had achieved in such a short period. Years later, however, he still cited his most embarrassing moment in football as being red-carded against Everton. Like Owen, Steven Gerrard is an intelligent footballer who has always learned from his mistakes.

During his absence from first-team duty, Steven Gerrard picked up a minor injury in training and he did not play for Liverpool again until the Reds' 3-1 victory over Bradford at the beginning of November. Liverpool's victory over the Yorkshire side set in motion a run of thirteen Premiership home games to the end of the season during which they lost just once. The Reds' away form may not have been great but at Anfield they were becoming a hard team to beat again.

Apart from the occasional minor injury problems, Steven Gerrard was now a permanent fixture in the Liverpool side. Playing on the right of midfield, Gerrard was now beginning to display his outstanding all-round skills on a regular basis. He was Liverpool's Man of the Match against Sunderland in November, a game that the Reds won 2-0. Some members of the press were even talking about Houllier's team as potential title candidates. The Liverpool manager remained cautious and remarked, 'To talk about titles would be very pretentious. Quality-wise and experience-wise we are not up to that standard yet. I am just trying to be realistic because I know there is still a difference between us and the top teams.'

Apart from Steven Gerrard looking an outstanding prospect, Michael Owen was also now beginning to hit top form. There were even rumours that Spanish giants Barcelona had put in a £35 million offer for the Liverpool striker. Whatever the truth, the rest of the football world were keenly watching the exciting young team that Gerard Houllier was developing at Anfield. Even seasoned professionals at the club such as Robbie Fowler and Jamie Redknapp were still relatively young players.

Liverpool continued their good progress with an emphatic 4-1 victory over Sheffield Wednesday at Anfield at the start of December. This game saw Steven Gerrard score his first goal for the Reds. The date was 5 December 1999. Gerrard scored Liverpool's third goal, a fabulous individual effort. The midfield maestro used his skills to the full to dance past three Sheffield Wednesday defenders before unleashing a piledriver into the Wednesday goal. The Anfield faithful had known for some time about the nineteen year old's potential, but this was the moment when he really announced his arrival as someone with all the attributes of an outstanding player.

Steven Gerrard's display against Sheffield Wednesday had Anfield regulars talking about him as another Graeme Souness in the making. Liverpool's two outstanding players against the Yorkshire side were both home grown (the other, Birkenhead's David Thompson, grew up learning the game on the Ford Estate, now known as the Beechwood Estate).

Despite the propaganda dished out on a regular basis by right-wing newspapers and lazy second-rate comedians, the vast majority of kids on Mersyside's council estates do not spend their time stealing cars and smoking crack cocaine. Most lads like Thompson and Gerrard grew up honing their skills and dreaming of the day when they might emulate their heroes and become professional footballers. When Gerard Houllier first took over the team his policy of signing mainly non-British players led to the team being dubbed Liverpool's foreign legion. Now, with the likes of Gerrard, Thompson, Matteo (born in Scotland but brought up in Southport) and Carragher in the squad the Merseyside link was becoming increasingly influential.

Gerard Houllier was delighted with the progress of his youngsters in the team and he could barely contain himself when asked about Steven Gerrard's contribution: 'When Steven first appeared in the team a year ago I told him that if he keeps his feet on the ground, works hard and doesn't get carried away, he should become a better player. He was outstanding against Sheffield Wednesday. He is not there yet, but he does have a lot to offer.' When asked could the Reds win the Premiership Houllier reiterated what he had been saying all season: 'I would love to say that we are a title threat, but we are not old enough or good enough yet.'

One aspect of life at Anfield that Gerard Houllier was confident he had changed was the booze culture. Former

Liverpool old boy Neil Ruddock had just released his auto-biography in which he stated: 'The great thing about the Liverpool lads, whatever the result, we would always go for a drink with the opposition afterwards and it became something of a post-match ritual that we would always beat them to the bar. We had a saying, "Win, draw or lose – first to the bar for the booze" and we invariably were.'

Houllier was determined to stamp out Liverpool's post-match drinking culture and he banned the consumption of alcohol in the players' lounge after games. The notorious Liverpool Christmas party was also now a thing of the past after tabloid exposés of drunken revelry by Reds stars during the pre-Houllier era at the club. 'An individual is like a top racing car,' explained Houllier. 'You can't say, "I'm having fun, training once a day and having a game once a week and also having booze a few times a week." If you don't have the right liquid, as well as the right food, it's just like a car if you put the wrong fuel in it. The engine doesn't work properly.'

Anfield might have become a less jolly place with Gerard Houllier at the helm, but everyone at the club knew what he was trying to achieve. As Christmas approached, Liverpool sat in fifth position in the table. Leeds were unexpectedly leading the Premiership, closely followed by Manchester United and Arsenal. Steven Gerrard had another storming game for the Reds in their 2-0 FA Cup victory over Huddersfield Town at the McAlpine Stadium. The third round of the competition was played in December during the 1999/2000 season because of England's expected participation in Euro 2000.

Former Reds legends such as Tommy Smith and Jan Molby were busy telling readers of their *Liverpool Echo* columns that Steven Gerrard was one of the most impressive young players that they had seen at Anfield in years. Smith saw Gerrard's future as a right-back. He told readers, 'As versatile as Steven Gerrard is, I'm convinced he can go on to play for England in this position and I certainly hope that Liverpool allow him to progress in his right-back role.' Jan Molby was equally impressed by Gerrard: 'He looks to have the potential to be an extremely special player at Anfield. Every time I see him play I am more impressed.'

The versatile Gerrard had already played at right-back, left-back, on the right side of midfield and in central midfield for the Reds during his brief first-team career. His favoured position was central midfield, but he was happy to play anywhere in order to stay in the first-team frame.

A good Christmas period saw Liverpool enter the new year sitting in second place in the Premiership table behind Arsenal, but defeat at White Hart Lane on 3 January dented their title aspirations. The Reds hit top form again with a fine 3-2 victory at Watford in their next Premiership fixture. Despite the fact that they had been deprived of the services of Robbie Fowler and Jamie Redknapp through injury for much of the campaign, the Reds were still putting in a determined challenge for a top-four finish.

At this stage in the season, England manager Kevin Keegan was now watching Steven Gerrard on a regular basis, with a view to taking him to Euro 2000 should England qualify. Gerrard's display against Premiership front-runners Leeds United in February 2000 did the Liverpool teenager's England prospects no harm at all. Playing against one of the best sides in the country, Gerrard was outstanding in the Reds' 3-1 victory. Leeds' team, like Liverpool's, was packed with top-quality midfield players, but Steven Gerrard outshone them all by some distance. Liverpool's victory was down to an outstanding all-round team effort, but the way that Gerrard tackled and sprayed inch-perfect long passes around certainly must have made Keegan sit up and take notice.

Gerard Houllier was delighted with his team's progress. He told the press, 'I remember we lost against Leeds in my first game as manager, but this time I was confident. We are developing physically, mentally and tactically. You need to be tough, but at the same time composed and calm and I think we are getting there.'

Steven Gerrard was a strong tip to be called up for Kevin Keegan's squad to take on Argentina in the 23 February friendly, but he picked up a knock during Liverpool's excellent 1-0 victory over Arsenal at Highbury and his chance was gone. The dejected youngster was given an assurance by the England boss that he was still in his plans for Euro 2000. Keegan said, 'If Steven Gerrard keeps on performing for Liverpool in the way he has been, he has every chance of being involved. He will get his chance, but he may have to wait until May when we play Brazil for his next opportunity.'

Gerrard recovered from injury to play a starring role for the England Under-21 team in their 3-0 win over Yugoslavia in a play-off to go to the Euro Under-21 finals later that year. The match took place in Barcelona. The headlines in the following morning's *Mirror* newspaper must have made sweet reading for Steven Gerrard and his family. 'Gerrard a talent Keegan cannot ignore,' wrote Harry Harris, who went on to report, 'Steven Gerrard staked his claim for a place in Kevin Keegan's Euro 2000 squad in dazzling fashion in Barcelona last night. Gerrard's tackling was crisp and decisive when it mattered. He also possessed the skill and vision to strike effective long-range passes.' England Under-21 boss Howard Wilkinson said after the game, 'Steven did very, very well.'

The delight of Steven Gerrard and his England teammates was marred by the racial taunts that Gerrard's new Liverpool colleague Emile Heskey was subjected to throughout the game. Gerard Houllier's capture of Heskey for a reported £11 million fee looked an astute piece of transfer business. With Heskey seeming a cert to become a permanent fixture in the full England side, Liverpool looked a side that would soon be packed to the brim with members of the national team. Steven Gerrard's display in Barcelona for the Under-21s had made him a certainty to win a full England cap soon. With his fame now spreading, the Liverpool youngster told Ian Ross of *The Guardian* that being the centre of attention on the streets of Liverpool took some getting used to. Gerrard said, 'I'm getting noticed more and more now when I'm out shopping or in town. I do still get a buzz out of people stopping me in the street. You have to be prepared and ready for things though. Things have happened to me off the field that I really never expected. After I was sent off against Everton, I had people being aggressive towards me. If you play for Liverpool or Everton and live local, I think you will get people spreading rumours and doing the jealousy bit.'

As Robbie Fowler found out to his cost, being a local celebrity on Merseyside can be a nightmare at times. Dealing with sudden fame was something that Fowler could obviously teach the young Gerrard a thing or two about. After a spate of negative experiences, Robbie Fowler had decided that keeping a low profile was the best policy, but even doing that was sometimes impossible. Fowler told the *Mirror*, 'I just want to play football and walk down the street without people looking at me, pointing at me. Over the years I've come to understand that it goes with the job. People who watch football think they own you. If they want an autograph they push a pen and paper in front of your face and say "Sign this!" There's no "please" or "thank you". Not everyone is like that, but the majority are.'

Worries about the trials and tribulations of fame were the last thing on Steven Gerrard's mind as he prepared for the remaining weeks of the 1999/2000 season. It had been an unbelievable period in his life, with full England recognition now virtually assured. Emile Heskey, feeding on the inch-perfect passes of his new Liverpool teammates such as Gerrard, looked a fine acquisition to Houllier's squad. He knocked in three goals in his first seven games, but then the Reds hit a slump in form. They failed to win any of their remaining five Premiership fixtures and finished fourth in the table. Steven Gerrard, still struggling with niggling injuries, was only a bit-part player in the final fixtures. Manchester United won the Premiership title for the second year in succession, this time by an incredible 18 points from runners-up Arsenal. Houllier's team, however, had shown a marked improvement on their previous season's effort and once again had European competition to look forward to in the coming campaign.

Steven Gerrard had been rested by Houllier towards the end of the season because of the young midfielder suffering from sore hamstrings and his chances of being in the England squad for Euro 2000 looked to be receding. Gerrard had made a sensational rise to the top during the season and his Liverpool teammate Michael Owen had championed his England credentials throughout the campaign. Owen had said, 'People ask is Steven ready for Euro 2000? In the Premiership you are coming up against top-class internationals every week. He has held his own against every one of them. At some stage Steven Gerrard will definitely be an England star.'

Steven Gerrard's Euro 2000 hopes had been given a boost in the spring when he became the first player to win the Cisco Young Player of the Month award twice in a season. The panel of judges, which included England boss Keegan, were impressed by Gerrard's performances for the Reds during March. A delighted Gerrard told the press, 'To pick up the award twice in a season is great and it has made me very happy to find out that I'm the first player to do that.'

Gerrard won his first cap in a warm up game against Ukraine on 31 May 2000. England won the game 2-0. Kevin Keegan was delighted by Gerrard's performance and the midfielder looked a certainty to be included in England's Euro 2000 squad. Keegan said, 'Steven is mature beyond his years, he is a great athlete and has shown he can perform on the big stage.' He did join up with the England squad for the Euro 2000 tournament, but injury limited his appearances to just one fleeting cameo in England's 1-0 victory over Germany. It was patently clear to all football observers, however, that Gerrard's future as an international footballer was virtually assured, providing he could steer clear of injury.

four

Make Mine a Treble

Gerard Houllier prepared for the 2000/01 season by bringing into the Liverpool squad German internationals Markus Babbel and Christian Ziege, Nick Barmby from Everton and Scottish veteran Gary McAllister. Other signings followed, including Pegguy Arphexad, Gregory Vignal and Igor Biscan. The promising young midfielder David Thompson was sold to Coventry for £3 million.

Houllier was bitterly disappointed that Liverpool had failed to clinch a Champions League place. He told the press, 'I understand the disappointment of not reaching the Champions League and it's a shame we didn't get the extra two points, but we have made progress. I have financial backing if I need to strengthen the squad more. The main thing is that everyone that plays in a red shirt gives everything.'

Steven Gerrard, like his teammate from the Liverpool academy Michael Owen, was determined that the season would be one to remember. Gerrard was now a full international and his next objective was to win silverware with his beloved Liverpool. Mixing with Manchester

United's England contingent at Euro 2000 had given the Merseysiders a taste for some trophy-winning exploits of their own. Owen remarked, 'When you join up with the England squad and you see some of the lads there who are playing in the same team as you, you think, "Hang on a minute, you've won six League titles and I haven't won any." The likes of Scholes, Beckham and the Neville brothers, they're always really good players. It's our aim to knock them off the top. We're all gunning for them. We get reminded all the time here that Liverpool doesn't settle for second best.'

In the coming season Owen, Gerrard and their teammates would still ultimately fail to catch Manchester United in the race for the Premiership title, but in cup competitions they were destined to become the undisputed kings.

Liverpool began their Premiership campaign against Bradford City at Anfield. A goal from Heskey gave them a 1-0 victory. A few days later they were brought down to earth with a 2-0 defeat away to Arsenal. In the early part of the season the Reds looked an impressive outfit on their home turf but away from Anfield it was a different story. The only plus was a stunning 4-0 victory away to Derby County, with Heskey bagging a hat-trick. Prior to the Derby game, Steven Gerrard had scored his second goal for the Reds away at West Ham to earn Liverpool a vital point, but in general Liverpool's opening months of the season were steady rather than spectacular. New signing Markus Babbel looked an excellent addition to the team, as did Gary McAllister and Christian Ziege after they recovered from injuries that had kept them out at the start of the season.

Steven Gerrard had been told at the start of the campaign that he would be rested from time to time. He was still growing and Gerard Houllier was keen to keep the young star's injury problems to a minimum. Speaking about this course of action, Gerrard told the *Liverpool Echo*, 'It's more precautionary than anything. I've accepted that I won't play in every game. That was the plan at the beginning of the season. As long as I'm playing in the majority of matches that's the main thing.'

Gerrard recovered from another slight injury to take his place against Everton in the derby game at the end of October. He had missed Liverpool's UEFA Cup victory over Slovan Liberec at Anfield a few days earlier, but was now raring to go. Steven Gerrard had had mixed fortunes in previous games against Everton, securing a famous 3-2 victory for the Reds in his 1999 derby debut with a goal-line clearance near the end of the game. However, his derby fortunes had taken a dive the following season with his sending-off. 'I definitely learned a lot from that red card,' said Gerrard on the eve of the game. 'That was the first time I've been sent off since I've been in the first team. Hopefully it will be the last.'

Steven Gerrard had an outstanding match as Liverpool crushed Everton 3-1, Heskey, Babbel and McAllister scoring the goals. Gerrard played at right-back and Liverpool legend Tommy Smith said after the game, 'Steven Gerrard proved once again why he is possibly the most exciting young talent in the English game at present. I'd go so far as to say that he is the best right-back in the world right now. Gerrard or Gary Neville for England? No comparison! It's a long time since I've seen a young defender tackle with such power and self-assurance. Wingers must hate playing against him.'

The debate on what was Steven Gerrard's best position would go on for some time to come. Gerard Houllier was delighted with his team's performance. 'My team went out and played out of their skins, particularly in the second half,' glowed the Reds boss. As for Man of the Match Steven Gerrard, Houllier said, 'Steven can play in several positions. At the moment it's better for him to play at right-back for fitness reasons. He had a great match. He's a big prospect.'

Houllier's plan to play Gerrard at full-back, where he could conserve his energy more and was less likely to put added pressure on his growing body, seemed to be the preferred course of action at this moment in time. In midfield, making the long surging runs that were a feature of his game, he would be more prone to picking up the niggling strains that could deprive Liverpool of his services for vital games.

After their derby victory, Liverpool were placed second in the table, just three points behind Manchester United. Everything at Anfield seemed rosy. However, was Steven Gerrard happy to be operating as a full-back and not in his favoured midfield position where he hoped to one day establish himself in the full England team? He said, 'I've been at right-back for a few weeks. I'm enjoying it and playing quite well. I prefer central midfield, but if I keep playing like that and stay in the team I'll be happy.'

As well as Steven Gerrard, new signings Emile Heskey and Nick Barmby were also a source of delight to the Anfield regulars. Liverpool followed up their victory over Everton with a fine extra-time win in the Worthington Cup over Chelsea. Goals from Danny Murphy and Robbie Fowler clinched a 2-1 win to send the Reds into the next round. It may have been a competition that the big guns showed little interest in, but Gerard Houllier, if he could not win the Premiership, wanted some kind of silverware at Anfield when the season came to a close.

Just a few days after the Chelsea victory, Liverpool travelled to Elland Road to take on Leeds United. Leeds had not made a good start to the season, winning just four of their opening ten games. Gerrard, having been dropped to the bench, witnessed a great all-action game which Liverpool lost 4-3. The Reds then went on to lose three more of their next five Premiership games. Once again they were displaying the inconsistent form that had dogged Houllier's first few seasons at the club.

In cup competitions, however, it was a different matter. In the Worthington Cup Liverpool followed up an incredible 8-0 victory away at Stoke with a 3-0 win at home to Fulham. They were through to face Crystal Palace the following January for a place in the 2001 final at Cardiff's Millennium Stadium a month later.

In the UEFA Cup, Liverpool travelled to the Czech Republic to take on Slovan Liberec in the second leg of their second-round tie, bringing with them a one-goal lead from the first leg at Anfield. Steven Gerrard had a fine game against the Czechs, playing in midfield in the first half, and at right-back in the second. In each position he was outstanding and was Liverpool's star player in a 3-2 victory.

The injury problems that had already caused Steven Gerrard to miss out on probable selection for the national team against Brazil, Argentina, Germany and Finland during the past few months now struck again. A hamstring strain, plus an injury to his groin, caused Gerrard to withdraw from caretaker coach Peter Taylor's squad to face Italy in a friendly. It was the same type of injury that had led to Steven Gerrard seeing little action during the Euro 2000 tournament. With Kevin Keegan having resigned in October, Peter Taylor was in temporary charge of the England team and would be at the helm until Sven-Goran Eriksson took over coaching duties for England's World Cup qualifiers the following year. Although he was disappointed to once again miss out on an international appearance, Steven Gerrard's injury problem cleared up and he was relatively injury-free for the remainder of the 2000/01 season. Liverpool were still cautious and rested him from time to time but he played in most of the crucial games of what would turn out to be an incredible season for the Reds.

Peter Taylor had been particularly keen to include Gerrard in his England set-up but he accepted that the Liverpool backroom staff knew what was best for the young star. Taylor told the press, 'I know Steven is very down and he's been very unlucky when he's been away with England. Because of the injuries he's had, it's been very difficult for him to play two games in quick succession. I'm sure the Liverpool medical department will be looking at the situation and I have every confidence in Gerard Houllier and their physio knowing about the fitness side and having his interests at heart.'

Although Sven-Goran Eriksson was to express his admiration for all things Liverpool during one of his first press conferences on getting the England job, Gerard Houllier came down firmly in the camp that wanted an Englishman to be appointed. Eriksson told the press about being shown around the boot room by Joe Fagan and claimed that the man he was replacing as England boss, Kevin Keegan, was one of his heroes as a player. Houllier was grateful to hear of Eriksson's admiration for the Reds but was still adamant that he was not the man for the job. He remarked, 'Sven-Goran is a nice guy and a very good coach who I admire and respect, but I still think the FA should have gone for someone who is English. We would certainly not appoint a foreign coach in France. There are plenty of decent English candidates out there and I really think that they would have been better appointing one of those.'

Liverpool approached the last months of 2000 hoping to see off Olympiakos in the next round of the UEFA Cup and then concentrating on their challenge for the Premiership title. The first leg of the Olympiakos tie took place in the Olympic Stadium, Athens. The atmosphere was expected to be intimidating and Gerard Houllier called for the match officials to be on their guard against underhand tactics from the Greek team. The Olympiakos manager Yiannis Moutzarakis took exception to Houllier's comments and told the press that a club such as Liverpool should be above making such allegations.

A fiery game was expected and Houllier decided to play Steven Gerrard in central midfield, with Didi Hamann playing the more defensive midfield role. Crucial away goals from Nick Barmby and Gerrard helped Liverpool to an excellent 2-2 draw. The Reds were confident that they could finish off the Greeks at Anfield two weeks later.

Steven Gerrard's outstanding performance in the centre of midfield opened up the debate again about where the youngster's best position was. Gerard Houllier remarked, 'I know you like to say, "He plays there and he can't play there." This is the attitude of forty years ago. Look at France's Lilian Thuram, he plays centre-back and right-back.' In Steven Gerrard, the Liverpool manager had a player on his hands who was equally impressive in whatever position he was selected to play. It was a problem that most Premiership managers would love to have as they cast envious glances towards Anfield's gifted youngster.

A feature of Steven Gerrard's growing confidence at this stage was that he was often one of the Liverpool players who was happy to be quoted after games. Giving press interviews didn't appear to faze him and his comments always appeared to be constructive and well thought out. It was hard to believe that he was still just twenty years old. Reflecting on his team's draw against Olympiakos, Gerrard commented, 'We came to Athens to play as a team and stuck together. Now we have to make the same effort to finish them off at Anfield. We played with a lot of heart. We've set the standard now. They were a Champions League team, but we outplayed them.'

One negative aspect of Liverpool's trip to Athens was the treatment dished out to the 500-strong group of Reds fans who were accompanied to the game by members of the Merseyside Police Force. The Greek police from the outset treated the Liverpool contingent appallingly and stood by and watched as concrete, bottles and other missiles were thrown at the Reds' supporters. When the members of the Liverpool Police complained to their Greek counterparts they were simply told that the Reds fans were drunken hooligans. One Liverpool Councillor, Peter Millen, who attended the game said, 'I have been to matches in former communist countries where you might have expected some heavy-handedness, but to witness this in a fellow EC country like Greece is just an outrage.'

The return leg against Olympiakos on 7 December was eagerly awaited by the Liverpool fans. The Reds warmed up for the game with an impressive 3-0 victory over Charlton at Anfield. Steven Gerrard was once again operating in central midfield alongside the impressive Gary McAlllister. Liverpool were now in fourth spot in the Premiership and had crucial games coming up over the Christmas period against Manchester United and Arsenal. Olympiakos arrived at Anfield with a new manager in charge after Moutzarakis was sacked after the first leg of the tie.

Liverpool booked their place in the quarter-finals of the UEFA Cup with a scintillating display of football. Heskey and Barmby scored the goals that gave Liverpool a 2-0 victory. Man of the Match was once again Steven Gerrard, playing in his central midfield role. Heskey's goal was his twelfth of the season and he was beginning to become a firm favourite with the Anfield crowd. Watching the game from the stands was Sven-Goran Eriksson's assistant, Tord Grip. Grip's report on the game to the new England boss must have had the name of Steven Gerrard written in large letters for once again the blossoming talent of the young midfield player was there for all to see.

Just three days after their fabulous display against Olympiakos, Liverpool slumped to an unexpected 1-0 home defeat against Ipswich. Steven Gerrard had been rested for the Ipswich game but was back in the side to play Manchester United at Old Trafford the following week. Liverpool were thirteen points behind table-topping United in the Premiership and a win was vital to keep up their spirits for the rest of the season. Former Liverpool boss Roy Evans was asked on the eve of the game if he was impressed by his successor Gerard Houllier's period in control at the club. Evans remarked, 'When you consider the money they have spent, Liverpool haven't made a great challenge to United's supremacy. The fans are disgruntled that nowadays they're so far behind. Gerard said he needed three years and I suppose he's only halfway through. That means there should be better to come.'

The pre-match build-up centred on Steven Gerrard's midfield battle with Roy Keane. Keane was a player who Gerrard admired greatly, but he was determined to come out on top in this particular encounter. Gerard Houllier knew that the Keane/Gerrard tussle would be a determining factor in the game. He said, 'I have no doubts that Steven will be as good as Roy Keane in the future. His standard of performance gets better and better. Even if we beat United on Sunday, however, they will still win the League. You might say that is defeatist; I say it is reality.'

Liverpool did go on to record a famous victory over the Premiership's top team in this pre-Christmas encounter. Danny Murphy scored the goal to give the Reds a 1-0 victory. Steven Gerrard was chosen by Houllier to play a more defensive midfield role alongside Igor Biscan. The United midfield of Keane, Butt, Beckham and Giggs failed to build up any superiority as the whole of the Liverpool side played out of their skins to keep the home side at bay. Next up for Liverpool was a date against the country's second-best team Arsenal.

Despite Liverpool's victory over Manchester United, the Old Trafford club were still expected to retain their Premiership title with relative ease. Former Liverpool star and now television soccer pundit Mark Lawrenson claimed that this season's Premiership was the worst ever. Lawrenson suggested that Manchester United's rivals were not putting up a strong enough challenge in their efforts to stop the Manchester club's virtual monopoly of the league. Sir Alex Ferguson's response was to say, 'The advantage we have is continuity. We have a settled squad who are maturing together, whereas Liverpool, Arsenal and Chelsea are still in the process of bringing in a number of players.'

Gerard Houllier was under fire by some Liverpool fans at this stage in the season for rotating his squad too often in an effort to keep his players fresh and injury-free. Sir Alex Ferguson, who was doing the same thing with his Manchester United squad, argued that Houllier was right to do so: 'You have to look at the big picture and that is what Gerard Houllier is doing. What do you do – keep playing people until they are dead on their feet? You have got to do it. Take Michael Owen: for a young player, he has suffered from over-exposure and Gerard knows that.'

Liverpool took on Arsenal at Anfield on 23 December 2000 knowing that if they could follow up their victory at Old Trafford with another against the London club their season would receive a massive boost. Steven Gerrard was once again up against one of Europe's top midfielders in Arsenal's Patrick Vieira. Like Roy Keane the week before, Vieira was another player that Gerrard had great admiration for. Gerard Houllier said that he was delighted with Steven Gerrard's recent contribution to the team's performances. 'He rises to the big games,' said Houllier. 'There was a time when Steven struggled to play two successive games, but that is improving and his overall awareness is also getting better.'

Once again Steven Gerrard had a storming game as Liverpool annihilated Arsenal 4-0. It was one of their finest performances in years and Arsenal boss Arsène Wenger said after the game that if Manchester United slipped up then Liverpool could be strong title challengers. Man of the Match Gerrard scored Liverpool's opening goal with a sweetly taken volley from the edge of the penalty area. Talk of a title challenge, however, was played down by Gerrard after the game. He told the press, 'Our main priority is to finish in the top three. Mind you, if we keep playing like that then who knows?'

After Steven Gerrard's displays against Manchester United and Arsenal, some members of the press were now describing him as a serious challenger to Roy Keane and Patrick Vieira's title as one of the top enforcers in the league. For the time being he seemed to be free of the injury ailments that had plagued his first-team career at Anfield. There was also the added bonus that Gerrard was now beginning to score vital goals for the Reds on a regular basis. He followed up a stunning thirty-yard goal against Southampton with another cracker against Aston Villa a few weeks later. In between these Premiership matches, both of which were won by Liverpool, the Reds also progressed in the FA Cup with a third-round 3-0 victory over Rotherham.

Steven Gerrard's growing goals tally meant that he had now added the only aspect of his game that appeared to be lacking. Gerard Houllier was even now talking in terms of Gerrard developing into a great player if he continued to score goals on a regular basis. Oliver Kay of *The Times* interviewed Houllier and asked him about the first time he had seen Steven Gerrard in action. Houllier recalled that he had been advised to check out two other players who were taking part in a Liverpool academy Under-19 game. The player who impressed him, however, was not the two recommended teenagers but Steven Gerrard. 'I could see very quickly that he was something special, that he was a special talent,' said Houllier. 'It was a funny situation really, because I was supposed to be looking at other players, but he was the player I saw. I knew straight away that he was the one I wanted. He was a different class.'

Gerard Houllier added Jari Litmanen to his squad for the second half of the season, securing the Finnish forward from Barcelona in January 2001. When everyone was fit and available, the competition for places in the Liverpool midfield was now intense. The fantastic form of Steven Gerrard, however, meant that he was now a virtual certainty to be selected. It had been a meteoric rise to prominence in the

Anfield set-up for Gerrard and his injury-free run meant that he would probably soon start to feature regularly for England too.

Dietmar Hamann was one of those Liverpool midfielders vying for selection alongside Steven Gerrard. He told Chris Bascombe of the *Liverpool Echo* about his admiration for his young midfield partner: 'Steven is producing top performances week in and week out. The main thing in football is confidence. When you have confidence you can play to your best and at the moment Steven's is sky high. The way he is playing at the moment he only needs half a chance and he puts it away. If he continues to progress in the manner he has in the last year he has a great career ahead of him.'

Liverpool ended the month of January with important cup games that could make or break their season. Crystal Palace came to Anfield on 24 January holding a 2-1 lead from the first leg of the Worthington Cup semi-final tie. Liverpool swept Palace aside 5-0 to reach their first major cup final under Gerard Houllier. Steven Gerrard was switched to right-back for this game after Markus Babbal was forced to miss the game through illness. Gerrard had a storming game at full-back, not giving the Palace danger man Andrejs Rubins a sniff of the ball.

With one cup final appearance in the bag, Liverpool went into a meeting with Leeds United in the FA Cup three days later. Steven Gerrard missed the Leeds match after picking up a knock against Crystal Palace. Inspired by a fit-again Robbie Fowler, Liverpool came through a tough tie against Leeds 2-0, Barmby and Heskey scoring the goals. Gerrard was back in the team the following week for Liverpool's Premiership clash with West Ham. Sven-Goran Eriksson was at Anfield to check on Liverpool's England contingent and also the up-and-coming West Ham youngsters Joe Cole, Michael Carrick and Frank Lampard. Two goals from Fowler and another from Smicer gave the Reds a comfortable 3–0 victory. The watching Eriksson was undoubtedly impressed by the red-hot form of Robbie Fowler but the way young midfield dynamo Steven Gerrard barely allowed the talented trio of Cole, Carrick and Lampard to make a mark on the game must have also impressed the England boss.

Gerrard's joy at now being recognised as one of the country's outstanding young footballers was further heightened when he was chosen as the Merseyside Sports Personality of the Year for 2000. Steven Gerrard was presented with the award at Liverpool's Moat House Hotel. He told the press, 'An award like this means a lot to me because it is voted for by the fans. A lot of people out there like how I play, which makes me feel very proud. When I look at the names on this trophy, it's a tremendous pleasure to be among people who are legends.' Gerrard was also keen to express his gratitude to the physio staff at Anfield who had played such a significant role in getting his body fit enough to play so many games in what had been a difficult year injuries-wise.

February 2001 was destined to be one of the most significant months in Gerard Houllier's reign as Liverpool manager. Catching Manchester United in the Premiership looked an unattainable goal; the three cup competitions that the Reds were still involved in, however, looked a different matter. Within the space of seven days Liverpool were due to play Roma in the first leg of the UEFA Cup, Manchester City in the FA Cup, then Birmingham City in the Worthington Cup final. Houllier and his assistant Phil Thompson would need their motivational skills to be at a premium to get them through this fixture list with their dreams of a treble of cup successes still intact.

It was like a scene from the glory days of the 1970s and '80s when thousands of Reds fans jetted out of Liverpool Airport for the away fixture against Roma. Steven Gerrard had to miss the fixture because of a groin strain, but even without him Liverpool put on a magnificent display to win 2-0 with Michael Owen scoring both goals. Gerard Houllier dedicated the Reds' fabulous victory to Liverpool's travelling contingent. He said, 'So many of them made the trip here and they have stood by us through thick and thin over the last few years. I dedicate this victory to them.' Once again Liverpool fans were on the receiving end of violent treatment from baton-wielding police. A reported fourteen Reds supporters also received stab wounds from marauding Roma supporters before and after the game. No Liverpool fans were arrested, despite the provocation they were under.

Within days of the Roma game, Liverpool met Manchester City at Anfield in the FA Cup. Steven Gerrard had failed to recover from his groin strain, but goals from Litmanen, Heskey, Smicer and Babbel gave the Reds a comfortable 4-2 victory. The return fixture against Roma was next for Houllier's team and a dejected Gerrard was forced to sit out another vital Liverpool game. The Liverpool backroom staff were confident that they would have him fit for the Worthington Cup final against Birmingham that weekend so Houllier decided not to risk him against their Italian opponents.

Roma manager Fabio Capello arrived in Liverpool confident that his star-studded team could overcome Liverpool's two-goal lead. They could boast outstanding world-class talent in their line-up, such as Walter Samuel, Gabriel Batistuta and Francesco Totti. One person who was particularly sad that Steven Gerrard was not in the Reds' line-up was Roma director Fabio Baldini. There had been rumours circulating that Baldini had sanctioned a £15 million bid for the young midfield star. Before the game Baldini remarked, 'The only Liverpool player that interests me will not play and his name is Gerrard. I have been aware of him for quite a while. He is one of England's best young players.' Although Liverpool lost the home tie 1-0 they had done enough in the first game to take them through to the UEFA Cup quarter-finals to play Portuguese side Porto.

Liverpool's next match in a hectic period of vital fixtures was against Birmingham City in the Worthington Cup final at the Millennium Stadium. Steven Gerrard returned to the team for this game and said that he was looking forward to his major finals. 'I was devastated to miss the games against Roma, but if I had the choice between missing Roma and Birmingham, I'd rather play in the final,' he said. 'It's a major cup final. It's not Liverpool's style to enter cup competitions and not try to win them.' Gerard Houllier was desperate for his first major final as Liverpool manager to be a victory. He may have still had his detractors but in his opinion the club had improved beyond all recognition. 'If you look at where we are right now, it shows a massive improvement compared to two years ago,' he said. 'If we win tomorrow it would be a significant boost to the confidence of the team. It will increase the self-belief of the players.'

Liverpool, as was expected, won the Worthington Cup, but Birmingham made them fight all the way. Robbie Fowler put Liverpool into the lead with probably his greatest goal in a Liverpool shirt. Latching onto a flick from Heskey, he struck a magnificent volley past Bennett in the Birmingham goal. Fowler was at least twenty yards out when he let fly with his wonder strike. Liverpool, however, were not playing as well as they had performed in the weeks leading up to the final, and Birmingham got a deserved equaliser from a Darren Purse penalty to take the match into extra time. By this stage Steven Gerrard had been forced to leave the action with severe cramp. Extra time failed to provide a winner and it took a penalty shootout to secure Liverpool's first trophy of the season. It might only have been the League Cup, a competition not always taken seriously by England's top clubs, but it was the Reds' first silverware in six years. Liverpool had played much better throughout most of the 2000/01 season than they did in the final, but their fans didn't really care. They had a trophy, and now they dreamt that the bigger ones, the FA Cup and the UEFA Cup, might also find their way into the Anfield trophy cabinet.

Apart from their pursuit of cups, Liverpool also had ambitions of finishing in the Premiership's top three in order to clinch a Champions League place for the following season. After the joy of Cardiff just a week earlier, Liverpool's 2-0 defeat at Leicester at the beginning of March came as a bitter blow. The team now had to pick themselves up for their UEFA Cup quarter-final first leg away to Porto. Steven Gerrard was fit to take his place in the team and played on the right of midfield. Gerrard had a fine game and almost gave Liverpool the lead with a thirty-five-yard drive that Espinha in the Porto goal tipped over the bar. Liverpool came back to Merseyside with a fine 0-0 draw. Houllier's team had already played 45 games in the season but there were few signs of fatigue from a group of players hell-bent on winning more cups. During the whole of the previous campaign the Reds had played only 43 matches in total.

Next on the agenda for Liverpool was an FA Cup sixth-round tie against their Merseyside neighbours Tranmere Rovers. Tranmere put up a spirited display against the Reds at Prenton Park but goals from Murphy, Owen, Gerrard and Fowler saw Liverpool through to the FA Cup semi-finals. Steven Gerrard gave a Man-of-the-Match performance for Liverpool in this all-Merseyside clash and pundit Alan Hansen was quick to praise Gerrard and his Bootle-born teammate Jamie Carragher: 'Steven Gerrard has been both versatile and impressive for Liverpool this season, as has Jamie Carragher, who has been an unsung hero all season for the Reds. Gerard Houllier can build for the season with these two.' Liverpool's reward for beating Tranmere was an FA Cup semi-final against Division Two Wycombe Wanderers. An FA Cup final place looked virtually assured.

Liverpool secured their place in the semi-finals of the UEFA Cup with a 2-0 victory over Porto at Anfield in the second leg of their tie. Danny Murphy and Michael Owen were the Reds' goalscoring heroes in an impressive team performance and they could now look forward to two semi-final games against Spanish giants Barcelona. The good times were back in a big way at Anfield and to cap it all for Steven Gerrard, he was selected to play in England's crucial World Cup qualifier against Finland. The game was scheduled to be played at Anfield.

England boss Sven-Goran Eriksson had wanted Gerrard to play in February's friendly match against Spain but injury had caused the Liverpool midfielder to miss out. Eriksson was delighted to now have the Liverpool star at his disposal and he told the press, 'Gerrard is an enormous talent, the complete midfielder. He is an all-rounder who can do anything. He can pass, attack, defend, shoot and head the ball. He has everything the modern midfielder should have. You can play him as the defensive midfielder, more offensively inside, or as an outside right. He can play almost anywhere.' After Eriksson's glowing endorsement of Gerrard it was clear that the Liverpool player would be in his England plans for some time to come.

England prepared to play Finland at Anfield on 24 March with Sven-Goran Eriksson making an impassioned plea to the Liverpool fans attending the game to not barrack David Beckham and his Manchester United teammates in the England team. A longstanding feud between the Liverpool and United fans went back years. Recent comments attributed to United's Gary Neville, describing his dislike of Liverpool and their supporters, had done little to help the situation. As it turned out, Beckham and the rest of the England side received a warm reception at Anfield when they ran out to face Finland. Despite the fact that the Finns had Liverpool favourites Sami Hyypia and Jari Litmanen in their side, there was only one team that the Anfield crowd wanted to win and that was England.

Steven Gerrard was delighted to be declared fit to play in front of his home supporters after a week of concerns about his availability for the game. Gerrard had even made a trip to France to see an orthopaedic expert in a bid to clear up his persistent injury problems. Eriksson knew that a fit Gerrard was vital to England and he allowed him time away from training to receive treatment. Eriksson said, 'I am not worried if a player misses a training session now and then. I think sooner or later his injury problems will be solved.' Steven Gerrard had been advised to give up eating fried food and tomatoes in an attempt to clear up his muscle problems. He had also had his wisdom teeth removed in his efforts to rid himself of his ailments.

On the day, Gerrard played his part in a hard-fought 2-1 victory for England. Michael Owen levelled the scores after a Gary Neville own goal had given the Finns the lead. The roar that then greeted David Beckham's winner put to bed all the pre-match nonsense about the Anfield crowd not supporting the Manchester United players.

England's Liverpool contingent were delighted to get the crucial England fixture out of the way and the vital victory put them in good spirits for their team's pursuit of its cup treble. First, however, they had to come face to face with Manchester United's England contingent yet again when they played the Premiership leaders at Anfield at the end of March. Gerard Houllier's team put on a fabulous display to beat United 2-0, Steven Gerrard scoring the first with a stunning shot and Robbie Fowler notching the second. Manchester United still looked nailed on for the title, but Alex Ferguson's team had been served notice that the Reds would be on the lookout for their crown the following season.

Liverpool finished the 2000/01 campaign in third spot in the Premiership, eleven points behind Manchester United. When it came to their pursuit of the cups, however, it was a different matter. Barcelona, with great players such as Rivaldo,

Patrick Kluivert, Marc Overmars and Frank De Boer in their line-up, were favourites to go on and win the UEFA Cup, but Houllier's boys took no notice of the bookmakers' odds. The Reds put on an outstanding display of defensive football to hold Barcelona to a 0-0 draw in the first leg of the tie in Spain. Barcelona believed they were good enough to come to Anfield and notch up the victory that was required on Liverpool's home turf.

Before the return leg, Liverpool had a date with Wycombe in the FA Cup semi-final. The Division Two club put up a tremendous display but goals from Heskey and Fowler gave the Reds a 2-1 win that kept them on course for the treble. Wycombe boss Lawrie Sanchez told the press that he was proud of his team. 'My players were magnificent and gave everything,' he said. 'They are devastated and there were a few tears in the dressing room.'

Gerard Houllier said that reaching another final would boost his team's chances of getting past Barcelona a few days later to reach a European final for the first time since the 1980s. Houllier said, 'We expected it to be a battle against Wycombe. They gave everything and refused to lie down. Liverpool, however, can beat anyone on their day. Now we want to reach the UEFA Cup final.'

Steven Gerrard came on in the Wycombe semi-final as a substitute for Nick Barmby. Houllier, with the forthcoming Barcelona game in mind, wanted to make sure that his key midfielder would be available. Predictably, it was Gerrard who delivered a pinpoint cross to Heskey for the Reds' winning goal. His ability to make a difference in major games appeared to be increasing.

As expected, Barcelona made Liverpool fight all the way in the second leg of their UEFA Cup semi-final. It was veteran midfielder Gary McAllister who won the day for Liverpool with a converted penalty kick after Patrick Kluivert had inexplicably handled a corner kick from the Scot. Liverpool held on for a famous victory that saw them through to the final, to be held in Dortmund. They would play Alaves of Spain. Gerard Houllier and his team were on the crest of a wave. The Liverpool boss said after the game, 'I know it means a lot to the club and the fans to have reached our first European final in sixteen years. This was a real European night here, we have beaten one of the best teams in Europe and we have the resolve, determination and belief to beat any top team on our day.'

Liverpool would certainly need all of the attributes that Gerard Houllier had spoken of to win their second silverware of the season. Their opponents in the FA Cup final, Arsenal, were the second-best team in the Premiership and were determined to end the season with a trophy. Liverpool were given a pre-match boost when Michael Owen assured the club that he wanted to remain at Anfield for many years to come.

Steven Gerrard's battle for midfield supremacy with Arsenal's Patrick Vieira looked to be the key to Liverpool returning from Cardiff with the FA Cup. Vieira was bitterly disappointed to have seen his team knocked out of the Champions League on the away goals rule against Valencia at the quarter-final stage and was now desperate for FA Cup success. Vieira said, 'I want very much to win the FA Cup. It is important to all of us at Highbury.' Arsenal manager Arsène Wenger remarked, 'Liverpool look very strong now because they have so many international players who can be rotated easily. If they don't challenge for the Premiership next season it will be a big disappointment to them.'

As anticipated, the 2001 FA Cup final between Liverpool and Arsenal was a tense, tactical affair. Arsenal looked by far the more likely to win and when Freddie Ljungberg scored in the seventy-second minute they looked clear favourites to take the trophy home. They had had three efforts cleared off the line and were denied a clear penalty when Henchoz handled the ball on the line in the first half. In contrast, Houllier's team had created little and the midfield battle between Gerrard and Vieira was being won hands down by the Frenchman. In FA Cup finals, however, the best team often fail to get what they deserve, and when a certain Michael Owen is in your side you are always in with a chance. Wenger's team might have outplayed Liverpool on the day, but Michael Owen's two late goals turned the game on its head and won the day for the Reds. The team, their fans and the watching nation could barely believe it, but Liverpool had now collected their second trophy of the season. Arsenal supporters wiped the tears from their eyes and stared at each other in sheer disbelief. Liverpool fans danced a jig of joy and began to look eagerly ahead to their UEFA Cup final in Dortmund four days later. Gerard Houllier admitted that his team were fortunate. 'We didn't really start playing until we went behind,' he said. 'As for Michael Owen, his goals were sensational.' Michael Owen told the press, 'We were desperately hanging on, but it's a case of not giving up. You can go for ninety minutes and not score and then it happens.'

Steven Gerrard admitted himself that he did not have the best of games and his honest appraisal of his battle with Patrick Vieira gives an insight into his desire to keep on improving as a player. Gerrard said, 'I learned an awful lot in that FA Cup final. For a start, I realised that Vieira was a much better player than me. It was my intention before the game to take control of the midfield and Vieira didn't allow me to do that. He's such a great player. He's so fit and he dictates the pace of the game. You can learn a lot from just watching him. In many ways he is a role model to me.'

With the second leg of the cup treble secured, Houllier and his Liverpool team set off for Dortmund for the UEFA Cup final against Alaves. Before they flew out, Steven Gerrard was presented with the *Liverpool Echo*'s Merseyside Footballer of the Year trophy at a ceremony held at the Moat House Hotel. The accolades were certainly coming thick and fast for the young Liverpool star and in a few days' time he hoped to collect his third medal of the season. As for his well-documented injury problems, he told Oliver Kay of *The Times* that he was growing increasingly bored with the subject: 'It's always a big topic of conversation and, to be honest, I get bored of talking about it. I feel I've made progress in that area this season. I can repeat games now, which is something I wasn't able to do before, and I'm confident that I'll be able to play more and more games as time goes by. You fellers talk about injuries, but when someone has played 41 games in a season and come on as a sub another eight or nine times, I don't think you can say they're injury prone.'

Steven Gerrard was fit and raring to go for Liverpool's game against Alaves, which they hoped would complete a memorable treble of trophies for the Reds. At this stage in his life, Gerrard was dating *Brookside* actress Jennifer Ellison and she had accompanied the Liverpool player to the post-match FA Cup celebrations in Cardiff. Boss Gerard Houllier was delighted to see his Liverpool boys toast their cup victory with lemonade and mineral water rather than the usual champagne. There was still another cup to be won and his team wanted to prepare for the climax to their season in the best possible way.

Football legend Johan Cruyff angered Houllier and his Liverpool team by describing their style of play as 'horrible' prior to the game. Cruyff said, 'Liverpool are like Bayern Munich. They are all about name and prestige, but in foot-balling terms they are two horrible teams. In my opinion a team is horrible if it is incapable of stringing three passes together.' Cruyff's comments were obviously influenced by the fact that his son, Jordi, played for Alaves. Jordi himself remarked, 'If Liverpool play with nine defenders, as they did against Barcelona, then Alaves will play with ten.'

Despite all the pre-match rhetoric, the final turned out to be one of the most entertaining games in the history of the competition. Liverpool and Alaves supporters spent

the hours before kick-off swapping shirts, songs and sou-
venirs and drinking together with not a hint of trouble.
The atmosphere before the match was fantastic and the
final itself superb. Markus Babbel headed Liverpool into an
early lead and Steven Gerrard doubled the Reds' advantage
with barely twenty minutes played. Ivan Alonso then pulled
a goal back for Alaves, only for Gary McAllister to put
Liverpool 3-1 up from the penalty spot. Liverpool's third
trophy of the season looked to be in the bag. Alaves, however, possessed incredible fighting spirit and Javi Moreno
scored two quick goals after the break to put his team
level. Alaves were now on top, but Robbie Fowler scored
an incredible goal in the seventy-third minute to put the
Reds back in front. Liverpool fans thought that was game,
set and match but, with just a minute left on the clock,
Cruyff brought Alaves back into the game with a headed
goal. Extra time provided yet more drama as Magno and
Karmona received red cards for Alaves, reducing their team
to nine men. The 'golden goal' rule was in operation during
extra time and an own goal from Delfi Geli, when he
inadvertently glanced a McAllister free-kick into his own
net, won the day for Liverpool. Liverpudlians at the game
and watching at home on television were ecstatic. Their
team had won the treble.

Gerard Houllier and his team were now up there with
the great Anfield sides of the past, for the time being at
least. 'Our fans have been the driving force behind us. We
couldn't have done it without them,' exclaimed a jubilant
Gerard Houllier after the game. The Liverpool boss had just
witnessed his finest hour in charge of the club. It would
not get any better than this for him during his Anfield
reign. On the Sunday after the final, an estimated half a
million people welcomed the Reds back to Liverpool on
their homecoming tour. The three trophies that they had
won were paraded for all to see on a bus with a banner
attached to it that read 'THE TRIPLE DECKER TOUR

BUS'. Steven Gerrard and his teammates had dreamt about being a part of such a celebration all their lives. Now, after their historic treble, they were the toast of the red half of Merseyside.

five

Germany 1, Liverpool 5

Liverpool had finished the 2000/01 season with a magnificent cup treble to their name but in the Premiership they were also-rans. Despite their having qualified for the coming season's Champions League, their massive army of fans throughout the world would never be satisfied until they were Premiership champions. Some claimed that the Reds were lucky to have won the three cups, but if the Premiership title was awarded to the team with the greatest fighting spirit then Gerard Houllier's boys would have taken that prize too – would have won it hands down, in fact. However, the Premiership is generally won by the best team in the league and Liverpool were still some way behind Manchester United when it came to that particular accolade. Perhaps the incredible cup campaign that the Reds had just enjoyed would lead to the massive improvement in their league form that would be required if they were to catch up with Sir Alex Ferguson's team.

Before Liverpool's England contingent could book their summer holidays for a well-earned break, they still had two international matches to contend with. At the end of May,

Gerrard, Carragher, Fowler, Heskey and Owen all played some part in England's 4-0 victory over Mexico. Steven Gerrard played from the start and impressed new England boss Sven-Goran Eriksson. 'Let's hope that he stays fit for Athens. He had a great game and is very important to us,' said the England manager after the game.

England were due to meet Greece early in June in an important World Cup qualifier and Gerrard had obviously been pencilled in to play. Eriksson was keen to play Gerrard and Paul Scholes in midfield, and told the press, 'Steven Gerrard is a very, very good player, but he will grow, he will get even better. Gerrard and Scholes are two excellent footballers. They have good technique, good shooting ability and are hard workers. It is not just that one can defend and one can attack. Gerrard and Scholes can do everything. Many teams that I've managed in the past didn't have players that could do that, but England have that.'

Steven Gerrard played his part in a solid England display in Greece and goals from Scholes and Beckham gave Eriksson's team a 2-0 win. Next in line for England was a tough trip to Germany in September, but first there were the opening games of the new Premiership season to look forward to. England's 1966 World Cup hero Sir Geoff Hurst was one of many soccer pundits who doubted that Liverpool could close the gap on Manchester United in the Premiership. Hurst remarked, 'This Liverpool side hasn't dominated anything yet. The teams of the seventies and eighties dominated football. Liverpool have had one terrific season. To win three trophies in one season is absolutely phenomenal. I think if they don't win the League this season, it's going to be hard to emulate the great Liverpool teams from the past.'

Gerard Houllier's two major signings at the beginning of the season were goalkeeper Jerzy Dudek and full-back John Arne Riise. It looked like the Reds now had a squad capable of mounting a strong Premiership challenge. Mention of the treble had now been unofficially banned around

Anfield as Houllier's team set their sights on achieving even greater glory in the coming season. Gerard Houllier was fully aware that closing the gap on Manchester United would not be easy. 'You have to say that winning the title will be difficult,' remarked the Reds' boss.

Before the Premiership season began, Liverpool had to make a trip to Helsinki to play FC Haka in a qualifying round of the Champions League. Michael Owen had a sensational game for the Reds, scoring a hat-trick in a 5-0 victory. Just as impressive was Steven Gerrard in midfield. Oliver Kay of *The Times* said of Gerrard's display, 'Steven Gerrard's contribution was equally as noteworthy as Owen's. Recently compared favourably to Juan Sebastian Veron, Gerrard was more reminiscent of David Beckham as he expertly earned himself space to send in a perfect right-wing cross that Heskey headed home.' Steven Gerrard looked to be in the same type of form as he was at the end of the previous campaign.

Gerrard missed Liverpool's Charity Shield victory over Manchester United with an ankle injury, which also caused him to drop out of the England squad for the friendly against Holland. However, he was fit to make a brief appearance against Haka in the return leg at Anfield.

Liverpool began the season with a victory and a defeat in the Premiership and a 3-2 win over Bayern Munich in Monaco to take the European Super Cup. The Reds had now won their fifth trophy in six months and Steven Gerrard and his England international teammates at Anfield set off for the crucial World Cup qualifier against Germany in Munich in good spirits. Sven-Goran Eriksson, at the match in Monaco, must have been delighted to witness German champions Bayern being put to the sword by a Liverpool side packed with England internationals. The omens looked good for the international clash.

In the days leading up to the Germany *v.* England World Cup qualifier on 1 September, Steven Gerrard used the pre-match press conferences to wind up his Liverpool teammate Didi Hamann. Gerrard told the media that during England's Euro 2000 game against the Germans Hamann had let out a loud squeal when the Liverpool enforcer hit him with a hard tackle. Hamann laughed off such suggestions, remarking, 'I read what Steven said, but I didn't squeal when he tackled me. He is no problem.'

Gerrard himself was determined to help his team gain revenge for their 1-0 defeat to Germany at Wembley in October 2000. Didi Hamann had scored the winner that day and the taunts that Gerrard had to endure back at Anfield after the German victory were not something the Liverpool midfielder wanted to go through again. Steven Gerrard missed the Wembley game, but the memory of England's defeat still rankled with him. He said, 'I sat in the stands and watched at Wembley and it was devastating – a bad day for the country. It would be nice to get one over on Germany because Didi rubbed it in a little bit. He was voted Man of the Match, so fair play to him, he played very well. Hopefully we can get our revenge then I'll do the same to him.'

Gerrard's teammate David Beckham also felt that England had some unfinished business when it came to Germany. He told the press, 'Losing that game at Wembley was heart-breaking for all of us, not just the players, but the fans. It made it worse with it being the last game at the old Wembley Stadium. We want to get our own back. We know the Germans have a fantastic record, but we are not daunted by it and records are there to be broken. Since the German defeat we have come a long way.'

England's team might have taken the field in confident mood, but the task facing them was daunting. Germany had not lost in Munich since Yugoslavia won there in May 1973. Former England striker Gary Lineker told viewers, 'They've only lost one World Cup qualifier at home in their entire history. England's chances are slim.'

An estimated 15 million television viewers back in Britain watched battle commence and it was the home team who took the early initiative. Carsten Jancker shot them into the lead after only six minutes. It looked like England's record of never winning a competitive international on German soil would continue. Fearing that this might be a humiliating evening, most viewers back home left the room to go and crack open another tin of beer or put the kettle on. They had seen it all before when England faced a big occasion. However, this England side was different; it was packed with outstanding young talent who were not about to crumble at the first sign of adversity. There was also the added bonus that four of the XI, Owen, Gerrard, Heskey and Barmby, were Liverpool teammates. They had just achieved a fantastic treble of trophies by fighting tooth and nail when the chips were down and they took this never-say-die spirit into the Munich game.

In Michael Owen England had a striker who was on fire and after twelve minutes he latched onto a Nick Barmby header across the penalty area to put Eriksson's team level. England's travelling fans erupted as Owen and his team-mates danced a jig of joy. Steven Gerrard had always said that since he was a schoolboy he had dreamed of scoring a goal for England. The thirty-yard thunderbolt that he blasted into the Germany net to give his team a forty-fifth-minute lead was certainly the stuff of dreams. It was Gerrard's first goal for his country and it is unlikely that he will ever score a better one.

England were now rampant and after forty-eight minutes Emile Heskey headed down to Michael Owen, who blasted the ball past Oliver Kahn in the German goal to put his team 3-1 ahead. The German team were now in turmoil, with the only noise in the packed 63,000-capacity stadium coming from the jubilant England fans. England's Liverpool contingent were now totally dominating proceedings and Steven Gerrard muscled Michael Ballack off the ball in the sixty-sixth minute before slipping a perfectly weighted pass to his Anfield teammate Michael Owen, who completed his hat-trick.

This was now turning out to be England's greatest performance since 1966 and memories of Sir Geoff Hurst's incredible World Cup final hat-trick against Germany came flooding back to older fans. Not to be outdone, Manchester United's England duo of Paul Scholes and David Beckham showed superb skills to set up Heskey for England's fifth in the seventy-fourth minute. The rout of Germany on their own soil was now complete. The shell-shocked German team managed to keep the score down to 5-1 as England pressed forward for more goals in the final fifteen minutes of the game. Their supporters had begun leaving the stadium in droves well before the final whistle blew.

Both German and England supporters felt as though the game was more like a surreal dream. Had England really gone to the home of German football and annihilated their hosts 5-1? Germany's goalkeeper Oliver Kahn said that his team would be scarred for life by the result. Kahn went on to proclaim, 'This is the worst thing that can happen to a footballer; the result was shameful.'

The German press described the match as 'a catastrophe' and 'the biggest disaster in Germany's football history'. In contrast, Eriksson and his team were acclaimed by the British media as national heroes. Eriksson said that his team had the ability to come roaring back from going a goal down in the early minutes because in Owen, Beckham, Scholes and Gerrard England possessed the world-class players on the pitch. Michael Owen, with his incredible hat-trick, made most of the headlines, but his Liverpool teammate Steven Gerrard was not far behind him. Gerrard had an outstanding game and even found time near the end to get his own back on Didi Hamann by selling his Liverpool teammate a double dummy – a real piece of footballing skill! Steven Gerrard's first goal in a full international for his country was also quite exceptional. 'I dreamed I would score and we would qualify for the World Cup finals!' exclaimed an excited Gerrard after the game. 'The goal came when Rio Ferdinand set it up for me. I hit the ball as hard as I could and Nick Barmby jumped out of the way. When it went in, I felt like running into the crowd. We showed a lot of character to come back from 1–0 down.'

Steven Gerrard had now played six games for England and had been on the winning side each time. He was England's lucky talisman and his fame was beginning to spread throughout European football. England's next opponents, four days after the stunning victory over Germany, were international minnows Albania. England completed a great week by comfortably taking the points with a 2–0 victory over the Albanians.

A few days later, Steven Gerrard was brought back down to earth with a bump when Liverpool were trounced 3–1 at Aston Villa. After the glory of Munich, Gerrard was now being portrayed as a villain after he was sent off against Villa for a horror tackle on George Boateng. It was the third red card of his Liverpool career and he admitted it was a bad challenge. 'It was a bad tackle, but I did not intentionally try to hurt him or cause him an injury,' said a contrite Gerrard after the game. 'I spoke to Villa boss John Gregory and George after the match. I felt it was something I should do.'

Despite hitting the headlines for all the wrong reasons this time, Steven Gerrard insisted that he would not change his style of play. He said, 'I don't want to be known as some kind of football bad boy. That is the last thing I want. I was made up to see George Boateng get up off the ground and carry on. I won't change my style of play, however. Aggression is all part of my game.'

Liverpool fans did not have to wait long for Steven Gerrard to make amends for his show of petulance against Aston Villa: he had an outstanding game for Liverpool in their 3-1 victory over Everton at Goodison Park. Kevin Campbell scored a fine goal for the Blues in the opening exchanges but Liverpool hit back when Gerrard blasted in a fabulous equaliser just minutes later. Owen and Riise then wrapped up the game for the Reds with less than an hour gone. Liverpool were once again the cocks of Merseyside.

Paul Gascoigne came on for Everton in the second half, but could do little to challenge Liverpool's domination. After the match Gascoigne was glowing in his praise of Steven Gerrard and said that he saw a lot of himself in the young midfielder. This was praise indeed to Gerrard, who had sat at home in Huyton as a kid with his older brother and the rest of the family cheering on Paul Gascoigne and the rest of the England team in the Italia '90 World Cup. Gascoigne went on to say, 'I think we are alike in many ways. I come from the same kind of background as Stevie and like me he just lives for football. It's all he talks about. I watched him playing for England and he is some player. I hope he is in the national team for some time.'

Paul Gascoigne found time at the end of the derby game to chat to Gerrard. He told him, 'Live your life right so that you can play in every minute of every game for England, and enjoy every minute of it.' Everyone in football hoped that Paul Gascoigne's advice to the Liverpool youngster would be heeded. However, within weeks of his outstanding performance against Everton, Gerrard made newspaper headlines when he was spotted out having a few late-night drinks in the week leading up to England's crucial World Cup qualifier against Greece. Gerrard had been over in France receiving treatment from an osteopath on the Monday before the weekend fixture and had been given permission by Sven-Goran Eriksson to rest at home on Tuesday before joining up with the England squad. The fact that Gerrard was spotted out having a drink with his partner Alex Curran near his home in Southport at 2.00 a.m. was embarrassing for Eriksson. He had already had to send Frank

Lampard home from the squad after the Chelsea midfielder was spotted having a few too many at a Heathrow hotel the day of the terrorist attacks on the USA in September 2001.

A few years ago, a top-class player having a drink with his girlfriend a full five days before an important fixture would have gone unreported. Modern-day football, however, has changed drastically. Players are paid big bucks and are expected to act in a more disciplined manner. Whether Gerrard had done a great deal wrong didn't matter; he had been reported and Eriksson was now in an awkward position. How could he have dropped Lampard from the squad, but still allowed Gerrard to play?

Despite pressure from the media to drop the Liverpool midfielder, Eriksson accepted Gerrard's apology, but warned him about his future conduct. Watching in the wings was Liverpool boss Gerard Houllier, who was desperate for Liverpool's image as a boozing team to be kept firmly in the past.

To most football fans Steven Gerrard had done nothing wrong having a few quiet drinks, but for the time being the damage was done. Paul Harrison, a spokesman for the FA, told a press conference, 'Steven Gerrard has given Sven-Goran Eriksson a full explanation of what has happened and he has apologised for any embarrassment caused. Sven now considers the matter closed.'

Gerrard was determined to repay Eriksson by putting on a great display for England against Greece. England knew that victory would put them in the following year's World Cup finals, but Greece were no pushovers. On the eve of the game Gerrard was asked by the press about his fitness and he said that his frequent visits to France had brought a great improvement. 'The osteopath that is treating me has changed the shape of my back and that has stopped other parts of my body getting injured,' he said. 'I can't train for twenty-four hours after the treatment because I have to let my body settle down again. I used to go to France every three weeks, but now it's every six to eight weeks that I have the treatment. It's definitely working and if it came to the World Cup finals I'd be confident about playing a lot of games in a short space of time.'

England duly got the point they needed to reach the 2002 World Cup finals in Japan and South Korea, but Greece put up a determined fight. David Beckham was England's saviour with a fantastic display. It was Beckham who clinched a draw with one of his trademark free-kicks in the dying minutes.

Steven Gerrard had a quiet game. Perhaps being put in the dock for the crime of having a few beers had dented his confidence. Always honest about his level of performance, Gerrard knew he had not shown the Old Trafford crowd what he was capable of. He said after the game, 'When we were losing 2-1 I thought what had been a bad week for me was going to turn into a nightmare. I spoke to the manager about what had happened in the week and he told me just to focus my thoughts on the game. Maybe what happened affected my performance. I was slow off the mark and my mind was on other things for some reason. Until this week I didn't realise how people will deliberately go out of their way to cause trouble for you. It was horrible knowing that I was in the papers for all the wrong reasons. From now on I'm going to start behaving like David Beckham and Michael Owen. They are the two best players in the country, so perhaps I should start behaving like them.'

The mere idea that someone would snitch on you for having a late-night drink obviously still rankled with Gerrard and in some ways he became suspicious when meeting Liverpool fans out and about in his home town. Steven Gerrard, after this chapter in his life, was never as relaxed as the likes of Jamie Carragher when it came to being spotted out in public, Carragher having the type of personality to take it all in his stride. Gerrard was now less comfortable about the downsides of fame, but he would have to learn to live with them. He was still a relatively young man and it would take time for him to become comfortable with the fact that he was rapidly becoming one of the most famous footballers in the country. Steven Gerrard, with England's qualification for the following summer's World Cup in the bag, now turned his attention to helping Liverpool make a determined Premiership challenge.

British football was shocked to its core by the news that Gerard Houllier had collapsed at the end of the home game against Leeds United on 13 October. As the Liverpool manager fought for his life at the city's Broadgreen Hospital, Merseyside football fans, both Red and Blue, hoped for the best. Houllier underwent a life-saving eleven-hour heart operation. The intolerable pressure that he had been under since taking the Anfield job had taken its toll.

A long period of recuperation was now needed for Gerard Houllier before he could even think about returning to Anfield. Assistant manager Phil Thompson took over the manager's role while Houllier recovered and, as was expected, he put in a sterling effort to keep things running smoothly at Anfield. 'Just doing the job for a week has shown me what incredible stress Gerard was under,' Thompson told the press after his first days at the helm. 'He puts himself 100 per cent into everything. His approach is incredibly hands on – he is probably more dedicated than any other manager I have come across.' Thompson hoped that he could keep the Reds in the hunt for the Premiership title while Houllier recuperated. They went on a twelve-game unbeaten run before coming unstuck away to Chelsea, losing 4-0.

Liverpool's first tilt at Europe's top club competition since the mid-1980s saw them advance through the group stages quite comfortably. Steven Gerrard scored his first ever Champions League goal when he hit the winner in Liverpool's 2-1 away victory over Dynamo Kiev in mid-October. On the whole, the level of Gerrard's performances had not quite hit the heights of Liverpool's treble year. The unforeseen absence of Gerard Houllier, his suspension for being red-carded against Aston Villa and being slated in the press for having a few late-night drinks had all played a part in Gerrard's temporary dip in form. 'I'm giving the ball away too much and I'm not as composed as I want to be on the ball,' Gerrard remarked at a press conference towards the end of October. 'I don't want to dwell on the England stuff, but I think there are a few people out to get me. I knew I'd wake up one morning and not-so-nice things would be written about me. The boss has told me to keep my head down and keep working because my top form will come back eventually.' After he had introduced Steven Gerrard into the Liverpool side, it was not surprising that Gerard Houllier's absence would be difficult for the young midfielder to come to terms with. Gerrard knew that Houllier would always be there when intelligent advice was needed about any aspect of being a professional footballer.

As Houllier's long period of rehabilitation continued, his team continued to do him proud. New signing John Arne Riise was looking an outstanding acquisition at full-back and the power of his shooting made him an instant favourite at Anfield. Goalkeeper Jerzy Dudek also looked to be an inspired signing and his shot-stopping ability was crucial as Liverpool progressed to the next stage of the Champions League. With Jamie Carragher also on top form, Liverpool's defence was looking even more solid than in their treble season. The omens were good for a successful 2002.

six

World Cup Heartbreak

Liverpool entered the new year in fourth place in the Premiership, just two points behind leaders Arsenal. The prodigiously talented Nicolas Anelka was now on loan at Anfield but it was Michael Owen who was among the headlines after scoring his 100th goal for the Reds against West Ham a few days before the old year came to an end.

Steven Gerrard was still not hitting the heights of the previous campaign, with injury problems refusing to totally go away. Gerrard opened his 2002 goalscoring account for Liverpool when he scored the goal that gave the Reds a 1-1 draw with Bolton on New Year's Day. Just a month earlier, Liverpool had looked a decent bet to make a determined bid for the Premiership title, but they were now dropping points at an alarming rate. Gerrard's goal against Bolton was a gem. The England midfielder charged at the Bolton defence, skipped past two defenders and scooped the ball over Jaaskelainen for an outstanding solo effort.

Caretaker manager Phil Thompson was concerned about Liverpool's habit of dropping points against the

Premiership's lesser teams and told the press, 'We've got to be concerned, but the lads have been great. I'd be more concerned if the effort wasn't there. We are not getting the rub of the green in some games but we are a very good team, as we've proved time and time again.'

Although Michael Owen was still knocking in the goals for Liverpool on a regular basis, Emile Heskey had lost his goalscoring touch. Heskey had only scored two goals in the Premiership all season and his form was a worry, not only to Liverpool but also to England boss Sven-Goran Eriksson. In the domestic cup competitions Liverpool had already failed in their defence of the Worthington Cup by losing 2-1 at Anfield to lowly Grimsby Town in the third round of the competition. In the FA Cup it was not much better, the Reds losing 1-0 to Arsenal at Highbury to end their interest in the domestic cups for another season.

However, there were still the Premiership and Champions League to play for, and with Phil Thompson in charge there would be no letting up in their pursuit of these trophies. Thompson and his team had stated throughout the campaign that they were determined to win something for Gerard Houllier. To achieve this goal they desperately needed to turn their Premiership draws into wins.

At the end of January a 1-0 victory at Old Trafford signalled Liverpool's intentions that they would put up an almighty fight to take Manchester United's Premiership crown. Danny Murphy scored the winner for the Reds and the victory put them just two points behind their Lancashire rivals. It was Steven Gerrard who set up the goal with a superb free-kick to Murphy, who latched onto it and lofted the ball over Barthez in the United goal. Phil Thompson was delighted with the victory but said United would still be in contention until the end of the campaign. Thompson said, 'No championship is won in January, but we'll be there, as will Manchester United, come the end of the season.'

Steven Gerrard was now once again displaying the kind of form that had made him one of the most talked-about players in the country. His Liverpool teammate Didi Hamann told the *Liverpool Echo* that it was Gerrard who was the catalyst behind the Reds' renewed title bid. Hamann remarked, 'It's no coincidence we have started to do well since Steven Gerrard returned to his best. Even when he isn't playing as well as he can, he is an important player for us. He can make goals and he can score goals.'

Gerrard was exactly the type of player that Sir Alex Ferguson would have loved to have at Old Trafford and the Manchester United manager told the press that he looked destined to become one of the world's great players, providing that he did not start to believe the hype written about him. 'Maybe there has been too much commotion about Steven Gerrard,' said Ferguson, 'The same thing happened to us at United with the likes of Beckham and Giggs. Players have to get as much protection as they can from their club. Steven is still very young. You have to wait and see how these players develop by the time they are twenty-six or twenty-seven.'

Just when everything was starting to go well again for Steven Gerrard, a recurrence of his hamstring problem put him out of a number of Liverpool's games in late February and early March. He managed to play in England's friendly against Holland before injury struck but Gerrard then faced a race against time to rid himself of injuries in time for Liverpool's final run of fixtures in the Premiership and Champions League. There was also the small matter of the World Cup finals that he had dreamt of competing in since he first kicked a ball. He missed important games against Everton, Galatasaray and Newcastle and Michael Owen expressed his concern about Gerrard's absence from the team, saying, 'Any team in the world would miss Steven. He's a world-class player.'

Liverpool managed to keep themselves in the hunt for the Premiership and Champions League with a series of solid performances, the most notable being their 2-0 win over Roma that put them into the quarter-finals of Europe's most prestigious competition. Steven Gerrard still continued to be plagued by injury. This time it was a groin problem that was keeping him out of vital fixtures.

By April it was clear that Arsenal were going to be the team to take Manchester United's Premiership crown. Liverpool fought to the end but finished seven points behind Arsène Wenger's team in second spot. Manchester United were three points behind the Reds in third. In the Champions League Liverpool were knocked out at the quarter-final stage by German club Bayer Leverkusen.

Phil Thompson had done a magnificent job in temporary charge of the team while Gerard Houllier regained his health, but for Liverpool it was ultimately a disappointing campaign. After the joyous celebrations of the unique treble season of 2000/01, much had been anticipated at Anfield, but to have kept the club running on such an even keel after Houllier's unanticipated illness was still in many ways a triumph.

As Liverpool's England players prepared themselves for that summer's World Cup finals, Steven Gerrard was desperate to prove that he would be fit enough to join Eriksson's squad. He played in a 4-0 victory over Paraguay in the middle of April and the signs looked promising. The Liverpool staff, however, had been expressing concerns about Steven Gerrard's fitness since February. The longstanding groin complaint was not responding to treatment and by the middle of May the news that Gerrard and England boss Eriksson had been dreading was finally announced: Steven Gerrard needed an operation to alleviate his groin injury and he would not be travelling to Japan and South Korea with the England party. Gerrard was devastated and Eriksson, who had already lost Kieron Dyer and Gary Neville through injury, told the press that losing Steven Gerrard was a major blow. 'To wake up in the morning and get terrible news like that – Steven Gerrard, Kieron Dyer and Gary Neville are all top players, they are big players for us, but I'm not the sort of person to cry about bad luck,' he said.

Eriksson might have not been the type of person who cried about bad luck but there were probably plenty of people in the Gerrard household back in Huyton who felt like shedding a tear or two. The World Cup finals only come around every four years and Steven Gerrard had been a certainty to be in the England team. As he sat at home watching his England teammates fail yet again at a major international tournament, his thoughts turned to Germany 2006 as his next opportunity to fulfill his dream of playing in a World Cup.

seven

Kings of Cardiff

As is the case at the beginning of every new season, expectations were high at Anfield that 2002/03 would be the campaign that would finally see them crowned as Premiership champions. Gary McAllister, who had had a fabulous couple of years at the club, left to rejoin Coventry as player/manager. McAllister, like a lot of soccer pundits, said that Liverpool must now be a great bet to win their first Premiership title. The Reds had finished runners-up in his final season at Anfield and with Gerard Houllier now fully recovered from illness it was felt that the prize was within reach. McAllister remarked, 'I really can see a big push for the title. There is a tinge of jealousy because I can see so much happening at Anfield this coming season.' With Steven Gerrard now fit again and Michael Owen probably the best striker in Europe, McAllister's optimism was fully justified.

Liverpool went to Cardiff for the Community Shield game against champions Arsenal determined to start the season off with a bang. Houllier's squad was strengthened by the signings of El Hadji Diouf, who had been outstanding for

Senegal in the World Cup, and French pair Bruno Cheyrou and Alou Diarra. Each of these three would ultimately turn out to be a flop for Gerard Houllier. The Liverpool manager also came close to bringing Lee Bowyer to the club. Many Reds fans breathed a sigh of relief when that particular piece of transfer business fell through.

Liverpool lost 1-0 to Arsenal in the Community Shield but losing to such an outstanding side early in the season did not worry Houllier and his team unduly. Steven Gerrard had eased himself back into first-team action after his groin operation in the summer. His main aim was to be fully match fit for the Premiership opener against Aston Villa the following week. Gerrard, like all of the Liverpool side, was determined to do something special for Gerard Houllier this coming season. He told the press, 'The boss is a great influence on all of us and it is really important to have him back. We want to give him something to smile about.'

Liverpool's opening fixture against Aston Villa at Villa Park did just that as a goal from Riise gave them the three points. Steven Gerrard looked to have fully recovered from his injury problems and, along with Danny Murphy, bossed the midfield. Houllier was also delighted with the performance of El Hadji Diouf on the right wing. 'That boy will run his arse off for the team,' Houllier told a somewhat bemused press after the game.

The Reds continued their good start to the season, embarking on a twelve-match unbeaten run, their first defeat coming at Middlesbrough early in November. Steven Gerrard's summer of woe was now becoming a distant memory as he settled back into the England line-up for internationals against Portugal, Slovakia and Macedonia. The Liverpool midfielder even found time to knock in his second goal for his country in the 2-2 draw with Macedonia.

England's game against Slovakia, which they won 2-1, was marred by racist chanting directed at Emile Heskey and Ashley Cole. Heskey said after the game, 'That's the worst abuse I've ever heard. The whole stadium seemed to be shouting and making racist gestures.' Ashley Cole said the abuse was unbelievable. 'Even the stretcher-bearers on the touchline were making monkey noises at us!' he exclaimed. Emile Heskey had also been subjected to racist abuse a month previously, this time in the colours of Liverpool, away to Valencia in the Champions League. Liverpool's black players, Heskey and Traore, were subjected to barracking throughout the game and Arsenal star Thierry Henry said that the problem was becoming so bad playing away in Europe that he was determined to walk off the field of play the next time it happened.

Liverpool's Champions League campaign in 2002/03 was in many ways a horrible experience. Although there were two emphatic victories over Spartak Moscow, the Reds failed to win a game against the other sides in their group (Valencia and FC Basle) and went out of the competition. They were then entered into the UEFA Cup, where they went on to enjoy a slightly more successful tournament.

Despite Liverpool's poor showing in Europe, one massive plus for Gerard Houllier was the form of Steven Gerrard. At the end of October Liverpool were sitting at the top of the Premiership, but defeats against Middlesbrough, Fulham, Manchester United, Charlton and Sunderland hit their title aspirations hard in the run up to Christmas. A rare defeat against Manchester United was acceptable, but the Reds' old problem of not being able to defeat the Premiership's lesser teams had returned with a vengeance.

Just two days before Christmas Day, Liverpool took on Everton at Anfield in a heated derby encounter. The Reds were desperate to take the points against their city rivals, but a fighting display by David Moyes' team earned them a 0-0 draw. Everton now had an up-and-coming superstar in their ranks in Wayne Rooney, and the precociously talented youngster almost won the game for the Blues when he shot against the crossbar with fifteen minutes left to play. Steven Gerrard was at the heart of everything that was good about Liverpool's performance, but he blotted his copybook near the end with a horror tackle on Gary Naysmith. Gerrard escaped with a booking for the two-footed lunge but the Everton team went berserk and wanted to extract retribution on Gerrard there and then. Gerrard apologised to Naysmith after the match, stating, 'I tried to explain to all the Everton players that I tried to pull out of the tackle at the last minute. I think it just looked bad because I went in with two feet. I did go in with my studs showing, but I can honestly say that I would never deliberately try to hurt a fellow professional. I spoke to David Moyes after the game and he said to me that these things happen in derbies.' Liverpool boss Gerard Houllier said, 'It does not look good. I will speak to Steven, but he said to me he didn't try to hurt Naysmith.' Everton manager David Moyes remarked, 'I've seen the tackle on television and I don't think it looks good. It's not my place to comment on these things, but at the same time players do have a code of conduct to abide by. Steven Gerrard is a fantastic player and I really admire him.'

Everton's point at Anfield kept them ahead of Liverpool in the table, the Reds being in fifth spot, seven points behind Arsenal. Liverpool continued to blow hot and cold in the Premiership as the early months of 2003 got underway, but in the Worthington Cup they fought their way through to another final.

Their opponents at Cardiff for the 2 March showdown were old enemies Manchester United. With Liverpool trailing badly in the Premiership and Crystal Palace having unexpectedly knocked them out of the FA Cup in the fourth round, the Worthington Cup was the only domestic trophy that the Reds could realistically aim for.

Football followers were once again looking forward to seeing how Steven Gerrard would fare against the midfield player that he had such great admiration for, Roy Keane. Blackburn boss Graeme Souness said before the game that Gerrard now had the upper hand when it came to the most complete midfielder in the country, 'Roy Keane strikes fear into people, but Steven Gerrard doesn't appear to be frightened by anyone. I haven't seen anyone intimidate him and he also has great passing ability and a great engine on him. He can win a game with a fifty-yard pass for Michael Owen to run on to.' To receive such praise from Anfield legend Souness must have built Gerrard's confidence no end.

Another former Liverpool hardman, Jimmy Case, also found time to heap praise on Liverpool's new enforcer. Case said, 'I see a lot of myself in Steven Gerrard. I watched him during his early days in the team and I used to think he shouldn't have gone for that ball. Now he's far better at timing his tackles and he's gaining valuable experience. He really gets stuck in and it's obvious that he loves the club. You can see in his face how upset he is if Liverpool haven't won the game. There's definitely a resemblance in our styles of play and also in our love of the club.'

Steven Gerrard was now such an integral part of the Liverpool team that if he played well, generally the whole team played well. Gerrard had an outstanding game for the Reds in Liverpool's 2-0 victory over Manchester United in the Worthington Cup final. He scored the opening goal of the game when his blistering shot cannoned off David Beckham's shin and over Barthez into the United net. Gerrard was winning the anticipated battle for midfield supremacy with Roy Keane hands down. Michael Owen sealed victory for Houllier's team in the eighty-seventh minute when he sprinted onto a through ball from Hamann and slotted his shot past Barthez. It might only have been the Worthington Cup, but United as well as Liverpool were desperate to win it. Just as there is no such thing as a friendly between England and Argentina in international football, the same sentiments apply to Liverpool *v.* Manchester United encounters in the English game. Gerard Houllier had now won another cup competition for the Reds. Everyone at Anfield was delighted, but in the Premiership it would take an almighty effort to finish high enough to gain entry into the following season's Champions League.

Liverpool were brought back down to earth after their Cardiff triumph by being dumped out of the UEFA Cup by Celtic. The Scottish champions looked by far the more accomplished team over the two legs and went through 3-1 on aggregate.

Just two weeks later the Reds travelled to Old Trafford and Ferguson's boys got revenge for their Worthington Cup defeat by thumping Liverpool 4-0. The season was ending on a sour note and defeats against Manchester City and Chelsea in the final two games of the campaign saw Liverpool finish a disappointing fifth in the Premiership. Winning the Worthington Cup was not enough for a club like Liverpool. Manchester United finished the season as champions and Houllier's team were still streets behind them when it came to maintaining a consistently high level of performance over a whole Premiership campaign.

For Steven Gerrard, however, it had been a magnificent season on a personal level. He was virtually injury-free and was the driving force behind all Liverpool's best performances. Gerard Houllier remarked at the press conference after Liverpool's final fixture against Chelsea, 'I wish I had a few more like him. He has been a force for us in midfield all season.' Gerrard actually received a red card against Chelsea for a second bookable offence, but Houllier refused to condemn him, 'What he did was out of pure frustration. Every team needs a player like Steven. If you think of Keane at United and Vieira at Arsenal, sometimes these players get into confrontation. That's what Steven is, a forceful English midfielder. He will get into trouble now and again.'

90

Liverpool finished the season 19 points behind Manchester United. Gerard Houllier told the press that his team were still two years behind the Old Trafford club: 'We know we are not at United's level. I think it will take two or three years to bridge that extra twenty per cent that is needed to catch them up.'

Two or three years was, however, totally out of the question for those that made the major decisions at Anfield. He was to be given one more season and if things didn't improve, Houllier was out.

eight

Captain of Liverpool

Steven Gerrard still had a number of important games to play for England in the summer of 2003 before he could take a well-earned break. First on the agenda were friendlies against South Africa and Serbia & Montenegro, followed by Slovakia in a Euro 2004 qualifier. Gerrard played in all these games, scoring his third goal for his country against Serbia & Montenegro. England scraped a 2-1 victory against Slovakia and, with a victory already achieved over the toughest team in their group, Turkey, qualification for the 2004 finals looked increasingly likely. With England's next qualifier not due until September, Gerrard set off for his summer break happy in the knowledge that in a year's time he would be participating in a major international tournament for the first time.

Liverpool began their preparations for the 2003/04 season with a tour of the Far East. New signing Harry Kewell missed the tour through injury but the rest of the squad made the long journey to a part of the world where Liverpool had millions of devoted followers.

Liverpool's first Premiership fixture of the new season couldn't have been more difficult. They took on Chelsea at

Anfield and lost 2-1, Michael Owen scoring for the Reds. A few days later Steven Gerrard was in the England team that beat Croatia 3-1 in a warm-up game for the crucial Euro 2004 qualifiers against Liechtenstein and Turkey. Back in the Premiership, after an indifferent start Liverpool gained their first victory of the new season with a stunning 3-0 victory away to Everton. Harry Kewell was beginning to look an outstanding acquisition and, along with Michael Owen, was finding the net on a regular basis. Champions Arsenal were due at Anfield in early October and that would be a game that would test Liverpool's title-winning credentials.

Before that crucial game, Steven Gerrard joined up with the England squad for the Euro 2004 qualifier against Liechtenstein. Victory over the European minnows looked to be a formality. Steven Gerrard had played nineteen times for his country and was still to experience being on the losing side. Liechtenstein hardly looked to be the type of opposition who would spoil Gerrard's England record. Everton's young striker Wayne Rooney was also now becoming a permanent fixture in Sven-Goran Eriksson's England team and it was Steven Gerrard who took Rooney under his wing and looked after him during his early days as a full international.

Unexpectedly, England struggled against Liechtenstein and it was only when Steven Gerrard and the seventeen-year-old Rooney began to display their incredible ability that the home team took control of the game. Steven Gerrard had a hand in both goals, delivering an inch-perfect cross for Michael Owen to head the first and then heading down to Rooney who coolly planted the ball into the net. Gerrard was desperate to avoid a yellow card, which would have put him out of England's next qualifier away to Turkey in October, and after his outstanding night's work was done he was taken off, being replaced by Frank Lampard.

England's 2-0 victory set them up nicely for the potentially explosive encounter with Turkey in Istanbul a month later. Michael Owen's goal for England against Liechtenstein was his twenty-fourth for his country, equalling the legendary Sir Geoff Hurst's international tally. Owen, however, told the press that he was pleased to have equalled Hurst's record, but that the main praise should go to his Merseyside colleagues Steven Gerrard and Wayne Rooney. Owen remarked, 'It's great for the city of Liverpool that our teams are providing important players for England. Stevie and Wayne are from similar backgrounds and have similar characters. People might say that I came from a quieter area, but we all get on well. I know that Stevie and Wayne have become really good friends now, which can only be good when we're all on international duty.'

Steven Gerrard, Michael Owen and Wayne Rooney had now become the basis of Sven-Goran Eriksson's England side, and if the national team were to do well at Euro 2004 and the 2006 World Cup, it was crucial that they remained fit, healthy and at the top of their game. The niggling injury problems that had blighted Steven Gerrard's Liverpool and England career now appeared, thankfully, to be a thing of the past. He was rested by Gerard Houllier from time to time, but he was relatively injury-free.

Liverpool welcomed champions Arsenal to Anfield early in October, but Arsène Wenger's outstanding side beat the Reds 2-1. Gerard Houllier had remarked several times that his team were still some way behind Arsenal and Manchester United and sadly for Reds fans that was clearly still the case. Steven Gerrard, Michael Owen and Emile Heskey hardly had time to dwell on their crushing defeat by the Gunners before they were whisked away to join the England squad for the forthcoming game against Turkey.

The Turks were always going to be England's toughest test in their pursuit of a place at the following year's European Championship finals. They were a quality team and were desperate to avenge their 2-0 defeat against England six months earlier. At the home game ninety-five England fans had been arrested before and after the game, which was played at Sunderland's Stadium of Light, and the FA were fined £68,000 for crowd violence and racist chanting directed at the Turks. A hot reception was expected in Istanbul, and the main fear was that even if England obtained the required draw to put them into the following year's finals, that crowd disorder could see them expelled from the tournament altogether.

When England took the field to take on Turkey on their home patch, three Liverpool players were in Eriksson's line-up: Gerrard, Owen and Heskey. Wayne Rooney had, as expected, retained his place in the side. The game was as heated and frenetic as had been anticipated and the atmosphere can only be described as a cauldron of hate.

Despite the provocation they were subjected to, the England team kept their tempers under control for most of the game. The 55,000 crammed into the stadium created a tremendous amount of noise throughout the game, but the only real moments of violence occurred when the two teams trooped off at half-time with the score standing at 0-0. Turkey defender Alpay was alleged to have insulted David Beckham as the sides walked down the tunnel leading to the dressing rooms. Turkish police were then forced to break up a mass fracas involving the two teams and officials from both countries. David Beckham said after the game that Alpay had clipped him around the ear and shouted 'F—— your mother'. After their bust-up Beckham and Alpay were warned by referee Pierluigi Collina to cool it and to tell their two teams to do the same. England held on in the second half for the draw that they needed to qualify for Euro 2004 and the players and manager were ecstatic.

Despite the fact that he had missed a penalty kick that would have given England a famous victory, captain David Beckham told the press that he was proud of his team. 'Passions were running high at the start of the game, but we stuck together and got our rewards tonight,' he said.

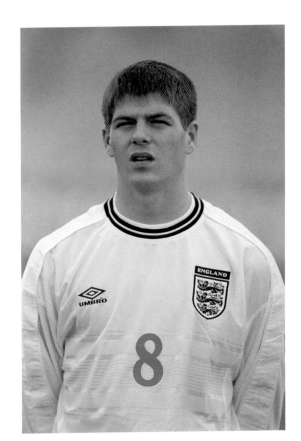

Right: 1. Steven Gerrard before the Under-21 European Championship qualifier against Poland, 1999.

Below: 2. England *v.* Ukraine in May 2000. This was Steven Gerrard's full England debut.

3. Steven Gerrard after being presented with the PFA Young Player of the Year award in April 2001. Also in the picture is the PFA Player of the Year Teddy Sheringham. Former Wolves star George Berry is in the centre.

4. Steven Gerrard tackles Jens Jeremies during England's Euro 2000 match against Germany. England won 1-0.

5. Michael Owen is congratulated by Steven Gerrard after scoring another goal for Liverpool.

6. Michael Owen, Emile Heskey, Steven Gerrard and Robbie Fowler celebrate Owen's first goal against Arsenal in the 2001 FA Cup final. Liverpool won the game 2-1.

Above left: 7. Steven Gerrard scores Liverpool's second goal against Alaves in the 2001 UEFA Cup final. In a fabulous game, Liverpool won 5-4 in extra time.

Above right: 8. A jubilant Steven Gerrard holds the UEFA Cup aloft after Liverpool's sensational victory over Alaves.

Above: 10. Steven Gerrard blasts in England's second goal against Germany during their sensational 5-1 victory in September 2001.

Right: 11. Steven Gerrard and Gerard Houllier applaud the Liverpool fans after an away fixture during the 2001/02 season. Reds supporters have a special affinity with 'Stevie G'.

Opposite: 9. Liverpool manager Gerard Houllier holds the UEFA Cup and Steven Gerrard the FA Cup during their team's triumphant tour of the city in 2001.

Above: 12. David Beckham attempts to block Gerrard's shot during the 2003 Worthington Cup final. The ball deflected off Beckham for Liverpool's first goal. Liverpool won the final 2-0.

Left: 13. Michael Owen and Steven Gerrard celebrate Liverpool's victory over Manchester United in the 2003 Worthington Cup final.

Above: 14. Steven Gerrard celebrates scoring England's opening goal against Serbia & Montenegro in June 2003. England won 2-1.

Right: 15. Liverpool have just completed a fine 1-0 away victory against Dutch side Vitesse Arnhem in the UEFA Cup during the 2002/03 season. Steven Gerrard applauds Liverpool's travelling fans.

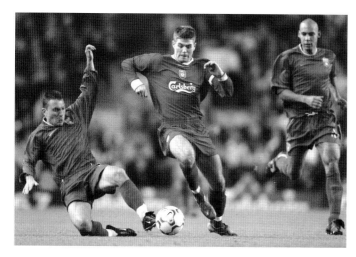

16. Action from the Liverpool *v.* Steaua Bucharest UEFA Cup tie during the 2003/04 season. Steven Gerrard skips through the Bucharest defence.

17. Steven Gerrard in action for England against Slovakia in June 2003. England won the game 2–1.

18. England players Nicky Butt, Steven Gerrard, Wayne Rooney and Rio Ferdinand line up against Turkey before the Euro 2004 qualifier at Sunderland in April 2003.

Above left: 19. Steven Gerrard celebrates his goal against Azerbaijan in March 2005. England won the match 2-0.

Above right: 20. A proud moment for Steven Gerrard as he speaks to the press after being named the England captain for the game against Sweden in March 2004. England lost the away match 1-0. Liverpool boss Gerard Houllier commented, 'I am sure that this won't be the last time Steven captains his country.'

21. Liverpool take on Olympiakos at Anfield in December 2004. A win was vital for the Reds to reach the knock-out stages of the Champions League. Steven Gerrard can be seen scoring the brilliant goal that put Liverpool 3-1 up and made the tie safe. Kenny Dalglish described Gerrard's strike as 'a stunning goal'.

Above left: 22. Leading his country for the first time, Steven Gerrard is photographed before England take on Sweden in March 2004.

Above right: 23. Steven Gerrard in action for England against Sweden in March 2004.

24. Frank Lampard scores against France at the Euro 2004 finals and celebrates his goal with Steven Gerrard. France won the June 2004 encounter 2-1.

Above: 25. The England team that beat Northern Ireland 4-0 in March 2005. From left to right, back row: Paul Robinson, Rio Ferdinand, John Terry, Michael Owen, Frank Lampard. Front row: Steven Gerrard, Joe Cole, David Beckham, Gary Neville, Wayne Rooney, Ashley Cole.

Right: 26. A jubilant Steven Gerrard punches the air with joy after Liverpool's victory over newly crowned Premiership champions Chelsea puts the Reds into the Champions League final. Magnanimous in victory, Gerrard said of Chelsea, 'They are a fantastic team with a special manager.'

Above: 27. After being 3-0 down at half-time, Liverpool's sensational fightback against AC Milan in the 2005 Champions League final is kick-started by this Steven Gerrard headed goal after fifty-four minutes. Liverpool won the game through a penalty shootout after extra time failed to produce a winner.

Middle: 28. Liverpool manager Rafael Benitez and club captain Steven Gerrard hold the Champions League trophy aloft after their team's fantastic victory over AC Milan in the 2005 final.

Left: 29. It doesn't get much better than this. Steven Gerrard kisses the Champions League trophy after his team's victory over Milan.

30. Two Liverpool lads who had dreamt about this moment all their lives. Jamie Carragher and Steven Gerrard parade the Champions League trophy around the stadium after their brilliant individual performances in the 2005 final against AC Milan helped Liverpool to a famous victory.

31. Jamie Carragher and Steven Gerrard celebrate Liverpool's fabulous 2005 Champions League victory over Milan. Like most top modern-day footballers, Gerrard and Carragher are on big bucks, but in many ways they are also a throwback to the days when Liverpool players gave their all for the red shirt.

32. Steven Gerrard holds the Champions League trophy aloft.

33. Liverpool take
on Welsh minnows
TNS at Anfield
in a Champions
League qualifying
round in July 2005.
Reds captain Steven
Gerrard shouts out
instructions to his
team. Gerrard scored
five goals in the
two ties against the
champions of Wales.

Steven Gerrard had another fine game for his country, playing wide on the left, and it was his run at the Turkish defence that won the penalty. Gerrard said after the game, 'We knew what to expect coming into this game and some of the lads have gained valuable experience playing in the type of atmosphere that you will encounter in the Champions League. We showed strength and unity and came through it and now we can look forward to the finals in Portugal next year.'

From the outset of his Liverpool career Steven Gerrard had always looked like a future captain of the club. When the Liverpool midfielder arrived back at Anfield from Turkey, Gerard Houllier informed him that he had appointed him club captain. Steven Gerrard was delighted to have been named captain of the club he had supported since he was a young boy and his first game as skipper was against Olimpija Ljubljana in the 15 October 2003 UEFA Cup game at Anfield. Liverpool won the game 3-0 through goals from Le Tallec, Heskey and Kewell. They would now meet Steaua Bucharest in the next round.

Gerrard's Anfield teammate Stephen Henchoz was asked about the feeling in the dressing room after the captaincy passed from Sami Hyypia to the young midfield star, a move that surprised some observers. Henchoz said, 'Steven is one of the leaders on the pitch. He plays with a lot of character and determination so it is obvious for everyone to see how much the club means to him. He will take a little time to become comfortable with the responsibility, but it appears clear to all of us that he is already enjoying the job. We won trophies when Sami Hyypia was captain, now we hope that under Steven Gerrard we are starting a new successful era in the club's history.' Steven Gerrard himself commented, 'Being made captain has given me a great boost. It's something I've always wanted, but I didn't expect it to happen at twenty-three.'

nine

It Could Have Been Us

Steven Gerrard looked forward to 2004 as the year he would finally get to play in the finals of a major international tournament. After the disappointment of missing out through injury in the World Cup finals of 2002, he was determined to make up for lost time and help England to win their first trophy since 1966.

The turn of the year saw Gerard Houllier celebrate his 100th Premiership game as Liverpool manager in a match that the Reds drew 2-2 away to Manchester City. Houllier might have won an assortment of cup competitions for Liverpool, but in the Premiership they were still some way behind the best. Once again it looked like the only salvation for Gerard Houllier would be in the domestic cups and the UEFA Cup.

By March, however, defeats against Bolton in the Worthington Cup and Portsmouth in the FA Cup left Liverpool with only the UEFA Cup to play for. Houllier was now under severe pressure and his team was desperate to win something for the man that the majority of them still had great respect for. Steven Gerrard, playing like a man possessed, had a storming game against Levski Sofia in the first leg of the Reds' UEFA Cup tie against the Bulgarian team. Gerrard scored the opening goal in a 2-0 home victory to send the Anfield crowd home happy. 'That one was for the manager,' the Liverpool skipper exclaimed after the game. 'He's had a hard time lately, so it was nice to get a good result for him. As soon as I scored I turned to the bench and saw how excited he was. It was just a natural reaction for me to run to him and share the moment.'

What with his match-winning performance and the fact that Steven Gerrard had become a father for the first time a few days earlier, his team might not have been in the best form but on a personal level he was definitely in great spirits. He and partner Alex Curran decided to name their baby Lilly-Ella.

The outstanding form of Steven Gerrard had been one of the few bright aspects of a disappointing 2003/04 season for Liverpool. They used to say that in the 1950s the legendary Billy Liddell carried the Reds practically on his own and at this particular moment in the club's history Steven Gerrard was doing exactly the same. In the away leg in Sofia, Gerrard once again scored the opening goal in a 4-2 victory. Liverpool had to play Marseille in the next round and the French team were expected to give the Reds a tough test.

Aware that Gerard Houllier was under increasing pressure as manager, Steven Gerrard decided to make his feelings known on the matter. He remarked, 'The boss is getting battered from all directions, but it's down to the team to try and give him a bit of a breather. He has put his faith in us as players and I think the time is now right for us all to share the responsibility and stand up and be counted. It's not fair; it's down to the players to get the results that are needed.'

Despite Steven Gerrard's rallying call to the troops, Liverpool continued to perform inconsistently in the

Premiership. On the eve of their UEFA Cup first-leg tie against Marseille, Gerrard spoke about the fabulous form that he was currently enjoying. He remarked, 'The birth of my baby has given me a huge lift and my confidence is very high. The goals have also been flowing – they say confidence breeds confidence and in my case that is definitely true.' As for the cup tie, Gerrard said, 'It's the only competition that we can now win. When you are at a club like Liverpool you are expected to win cups and all the team are confident that we can win this cup because we did it three years ago.'

Liverpool's first game against Marseille ended in a 1-1 draw, Milan Baros scoring the Reds' goal. If Liverpool were not to end the season empty-handed, an outstanding effort would be required in the away leg two weeks later. The Liverpool team were somewhat surprised to hear the Marseille team cheering when they got back to their dressing room at Anfield and were determined to make it clear in France that the tie was far from over.

Gerard Houllier, being an intelligent man, obviously knew that his days at Anfield were numbered as he flew out with his team for the away game against Marseille. The team travelled to France on the back of a disappointing 2-0 defeat at Southampton. He found time to praise Steven Gerrard before the Marseille game, stating, 'We must keep fighting and keep believing. It is always my belief that if everyone's attitude is right, then results will follow. The attitude of Steven Gerrard has been spot on. He is not only a good leader, he makes things happen and we all need to make something happen against Marseille.'

Liverpool's UEFA Cup hopes ended with a 2-1 defeat against Marseille in France. The only thing left for the Reds to play for was a Champions League place. Fourth spot in the Premiership would be sufficient and, despite an indifferent end-of-season run, Liverpool did manage to cling on. In the final Premiership game of the campaign, Liverpool took on

Newcastle at Anfield. The Reds had already secured their place in the following season's Champions League. Steven Gerrard said he was disappointed with only finishing in fourth place, but the chance to play in the Champions League the following season excited him. He said, 'There will always be expectancy at this club. I'm a fan myself and I want to be challenging for the top honours. At least we know that we are going to be playing the best sides in Europe next season.'

It was inevitable that Gerard Houllier would no longer be in charge at Anfield after yet another disappointing campaign and after his dismissal it was an open secret that Valencia boss Rafael Benitez would be taking over as manager within weeks.

Steven Gerrard joined up with Sven-Goran Eriksson's England squad to prepare for Euro 2004 in great physical and mental form. Despite Liverpool's poor season, his own performances now saw him acclaimed as one of Europe's top midfield players. In March he had even been given the accolade of captaining his country for the first time against Sweden in England's 1-0 defeat. In the absence of David Beckham, the England boss made Steven Gerrard captain for the game. Eriksson had remarked at a pre-match press conference, 'I remember when I met Steven Gerrard for the first time. If I compare the man now to the young boy that I first met, he has progressed enormously.'

That defeat in the friendly against Sweden was the first time that Gerrard had been on the losing side for England after 22 international appearances. England had two warm-up games for the championships, against Japan and Iceland. England drew 1-1 in the first game and then thrashed Iceland 6-1. Next in line for England was their opening match of Euro 2004 against European champions France.

As the football world eagerly waited for the game to take place, a lot of media attention centered on England's up-and-coming star Wayne Rooney. Interviewed at England's training camp, Rooney was quick to praise the help he had received from Steven Gerrard when he had first forced his way into the international set-up. Rooney said, 'All the lads have been brilliant, but Steven Gerrard is a good mate of mine now. When I first came into the squad he helped me out a lot in particular – little things like inviting me downstairs for a game of pool so I wasn't stuck in my room.' Chelsea's Frank Lampard also declared his admiration for Steven Gerrard, saying, 'The way Steven has performed in the Premiership this season, he has to be up there with the best players in Europe. He is a fantastic player.'

One of the teams expected to challenge strongly for Euro 2004 was Holland. Their goalkeeper, Sander Westerveld, told the press that all of the Dutch team admired and respected Steven Gerrard. He said, 'Steven is an excellent player, someone who is held in highest regard. I spoke to Edgar Davids and some of our other players. They all talked about how much they admire him. If he can carry on for a few more years without picking up injuries he will become one of the best midfielders in the world. I have played with the national team and watched a lot of European football, but Steven Gerrard stood out from the rest.'

As the England team prepared for their first game, against France, BBC soccer pundit Mark Lawrenson stirred things up by declaring that Henry and Zidane were the best in the world and that Beckham and Rooney wouldn't have a chance of getting in their team. As for Steven Gerrard, Lawrenson commented, 'Gerrard is now coming into his own and perhaps this will be his big tournament when he really comes of age. But he must show patience and realise that you do not always have to deliver the killer ball in the first minute.'

Sven-Goran Eriksson said that he had no worries about taking on France. 'We shouldn't have a complex about play-ing against these people,' he said. 'Our players take on Henry, Vieira and Pires every week in the Premiership. We won't be in awe of them. We will go into the game believing that we are at their level.'

Steven Gerrard was selected by Eriksson to play on the left of midfield, where it was hoped the Liverpool enforcer would nullify France's Patrick Vieira. The game lived up to its billing as potentially the game of the tournament. England were not overawed by the reigning champions and Wayne Rooney gave the French defence nightmares every time he received the ball. Frank Lampard headed England into the lead from a Beckham free-kick after thirty-eight minutes and France were relieved to go in at half-time only one goal down. The French danger men, Zidane and Henry, were kept well under control by the England defence, where Ledley King looked outstanding.

England ran out for the second half hoping for more of the same. Once again Wayne Rooney terrorised the French defence and when Silvestre was forced to bring him down in the seventy-second minute Beckham should have secured victory from the resulting spot kick. Barthez in the French goal kept his side in the game with a fine save from his former Manchester United teammate's penalty.

Just when it looked like England would hang on for a famous victory, Zidane was brought down by Heskey on the edge of the penalty area. Getting to his feet, the French genius lifted his free-kick over the wall and past goalkeeper David James into the bottom corner of the net. England were stunned. Then, Steven Gerrard made probably the first significant mistake of his England career. He failed to look up before hitting a back pass to David James. Henry latched on to the poor ball and, as the striker went to take the ball around James, the England goalkeeper brought him down. Zidane stepped up to put France level from his penalty kick. Steven Gerrard hung his head in shame at his one moment of poor play in the whole game, but players of the calibre of Thierry Henry only need once chance and generally they will make you pay.

France had snatched victory from the jaws of defeat. England had seemed to have had the game won before Zinedine Zidane turned the game on its head. The England fans were devastated. David Beckham said, 'All the team are sitting in the dressing room wondering what happened in the last minute. That's football and I'll move on. We've now got to win our next two games, but we've got the quality to recover.'

Steven Gerrard held his hands up and apologised for his mistake. 'I'm sorry,' he said, 'I just didn't see Henry and individual errors have cost us against the best team in the world. I'll make it up in our next game. I'm sure we'll bounce back.'

As the England team prepared for their crucial fixture against Switzerland, Liverpool, as expected, announced that Rafael Benitez was to be their new manager. Benitez had proved himself to be an outstanding manager at Valencia, winning two La Liga titles, and most Reds fans were happy with the appointment. For Steven Gerrard, however, his future was uncertain. He had formed a close relationship with departing boss Gerard Houllier and had put a great deal of his rise to the top of British football down to the advice, guidance and encouragement he had received from Houllier. Would Anfield be the same now that his mentor had gone?

There was also the fact that the Liverpool midfielder was beginning to form a formidable on-field midfield partnership with Frank Lampard and an off-field friendship with the Chelsea star as well. Steven Gerrard may have loved Liverpool Football Club, but the opportunity to double one's earnings by moving elsewhere would turn anyone's head. For the time being, however, Gerrard and his England teammates concentrated on the forthcoming match against Switzerland.

England knew they had to win against Switzerland to stand a realistic chance of progressing to the Euro 2004

quarter-finals. The players felt that the diamond forma-
tion Sven-Goran Eriksson wanted them to use against
Switzerland was not a system that they were comfortable with. Captain David Beckham and Steven Gerrard
expressed their concerns to assistant coach Steve McClaren,
telling him that they would feel far more at home using
the 4-4-2 system that they had employed against France.
Eriksson called Beckham, Gerrard, Scholes and Lampard
together and he asked them to vote on the system they preferred to play. The result was three to one in favour of 4-4-2,
Paul Scholes being the only dissenter because he preferred
to play in the 'hole' behind the strikers. Democracy pre-
vailed and Eriksson allowed his team to use a 4-4-2 system
against the Swiss from the start. The team took the field
in a confident mood. They had played well against France,
now they wanted some points on board in their pursuit of
a quarter-final place.

 England *v*. Switzerland on 17 June 2004 was the day
that the rest of Europe found out that the English possessed an eighteen-year-old who just might become the
greatest European player since Zinedine Zidane. Rooney
was sensational against the Swiss and practically won the
game single-handed. England did not play as well as they
had against France, but it didn't matter; Rooney probably
could have beat Switzerland on his own.

 Wayne Rooney scored two goals and Steven Gerrard
the other in a 3-0 victory. Rooney's goals made him the
youngest player to score in the European Championship
finals and the England supporters in the stadium, and the
millions watching on television back home, went Rooney
crazy. Beating Switzerland was hardly world-shattering
news, but it was the manner in which Rooney played and
took his goals that was sensational.

 Steven Gerrard was Rooney's closest friend in the England
camp and he was delighted by his fellow Liverpudlian's
display. Gerrard told the press, 'I could go on about Wayne

all day because he's a big, big talent. He's proven today that he's going to be a massively important player for England in the future. He's only eighteen and he's running international defences ragged. He's got a lot of experienced players around him to do his worrying for him. He's so relaxed, he plays like he has got nothing to lose. We need another massive performance now from Wayne against Croatia.'

As England celebrated their comprehensive victory over Switzerland, rumours still persisted that Steven Gerrard was about to sign for Chelsea for a £30 million fee. Chelsea's billionaire backer, Roman Abramovich, had moored his luxury yacht in Lisbon harbour and there was newspaper speculation that Gerrard had been offered £125,000 a week to sign for the London club. Sven-Goran Eriksson, feeling that all the transfer speculation surrounding not only Gerrard but also Wayne Rooney could unsettle the players, banned players' agents from the England hotel.

The *Liverpool Echo* printed a front-page story with the headline 'HANDS OFF! THEY'RE OURS!' warning Europe's wealthiest teams to keep away from Merseyside's fantastic young players. The *Echo*'s football correspondent, Philip McNulty, stated that 'Even at £80 million the pair for Rooney and Gerrard, this would represent bad business for our two clubs in terms of hope and morale of fans, seeing the clubs' two icons spirited away to a circus.' The circus that McNulty was referring to was of course Abramovich's Chelsea.

The rumours regarding Gerrard and Rooney's future were destined to run for most of the summer months. Apart from the allegations that Frank Lampard was urging Steven Gerrard to join him at Chelsea, Lampard's teammate John Terry was also quoted in the press as saying that Wayne Rooney should be signed by the London club as soon as possible. Terry remarked, 'I'd love to get him to Chelsea. I'll have to put in a word. I've not got the money to buy him, but I think there are others at the club who might.'

After England's victory over Switzerland bookmakers installed them as 6-1 third favourites to win Euro 2004. The whole nation now seemed to be behind them as football fever swept the country. Croatia had looked impressive in their 2-2 draw against France and England would have to be at their best to make the quarter-finals.

Wayne Rooney was once again the star of the show as England beat Croatia 4-2. Croatia took a surprise lead but, driven on by the outstanding Gerrard, England equalised through Paul Scholes. Unbelievably, Wayne Rooney then blasted England into a half-time lead with just seconds to go to the interval. Goals from Rooney and Lampard in the second half enabled England to finish the game 4-2 winners, Igor Tudor scoring Croatia's second. Once again Wayne Rooney was the talk of the tournament. Steven Gerrard was delighted for his young teammate and said, 'There's a lot of Scouse pride from my point of view as well. I know Wayne's an Evertonian, but it's always great to see Scousers doing well for their country.' Portugal were next in line for Eriksson's side and, although the host nation would be a tough nut to crack, Gerrard and company were confident that they would reach the semi-finals.

One unpleasant moment in what had been a wonderful tournament for Steven Gerrard was when Switzerland striker Alexander Frei was found guilty of spitting at Gerrard during his side's 3-1 defeat against England. The offence occurred while Gerrard had his back turned but television cameras picked up the offence. Frei received a ban for his misdemeanour and the Swiss FA showed their disgust at his behaviour by refusing to represent their player at the UEFA hearing.

With England's qualification for the quarter-finals assured, Steven Gerrard had a visitor at the England hotel as he relaxed with his teammates and prepared for their game against Portugal. New Liverpool manager Rafael Benitez decided to fly out to Portugal to hold talks with

Steven Gerrard, Michael Owen and Jamie Carragher to introduce himself to them and also to discuss their futures at the club.

It was obvious that Carragher was happy at Anfield and had no thoughts about leaving for pastures new. Steven Gerrard and Michael Owen, however, were a different matter. Benitez was desperate for the two of them to stay at the club, but the feeling on Merseyside was that neither would be at Anfield for the coming season. Deep down, Liverpool fans suspected that Michael Owen had probably played his last game for the Reds, but to lose Steven Gerrard would be a bitter blow. He had become an icon at Anfield, a player that the new boss could build a team around. Rumours persisted that he had already agreed to sign for Chelsea. Benitez left the England team hotel none the wiser about where Gerrard and Owen would be displaying their outstanding ability in the forthcoming campaign. The general consensus was that Gerrard and Owen would wait until Euro 2004 was over and then make decisions about the future.

For Steven Gerrard, the departure of Gerard Houllier and his assistant Phil Thompson meant that he would be returning to a different Anfield than the one that he had spent all his formative years as a player at. Perhaps for him it was the right time to go. Thoughts of transfer activity had to be put to the back of his mind as he prepared for the biggest game of his international career against Portugal.

England's chances of progressing to the semi-finals of Euro 2004 ended in the twenty-seventh minute of their game against Portugal. From the moment Jorge Andrade trod on Wayne Rooney's right foot, breaking a bone, England were as good as out of the tournament. Eriksson's team never recovered from the blow of Rooney having to limp out of the action and despite a spirited, fighting performance it somehow seemed inevitable that they were not going to emerge as winners. Portugal reached the semis after a penalty shootout, David Beckham once again missing from the spot.

They had begun the game in great style, Michael Owen putting them into a third-minute lead. Wayne Rooney had looked like he would increase England's advantage as soon as the right opportunity presented itself. Once Rooney limped out of the game, however, Eriksson's team went into their shell. Their teenage talisman had gone, now all they could do was try to hang on for a 1-0 victory. Portugal equalised in the eightieth minute through Helder Postiga. In extra time, Rui Costa shot the home team into the lead, only for Lampard to equalise. Beckham's penalty shootout miss, together with a similar failure from Darius Vassell, saw Portugal take the tie and sent Eriksson's dejected team back home to face a media inquiry over what went wrong.

If Rooney had not broken his foot it is highly likely that England would have come very close to winning their first major tournament since the 1966 World Cup. Football, however, is full of ifs and buts and the facts are that Greece won Euro 2004 and in doing so created one of the biggest upsets in international football history.

Steven Gerrard had had a magnificent tournament and looked every inch one of Europe's top midfielders. It was small wonder that when Gerrard arrived back in Liverpool Rafael Benitez would have one hell of a job on his hands to keep him at the club.

ten

The Reds' Turkish Delight

Steven Gerrard arrived back home from the drama and excitement of participating in an enthralling European Championship knowing that he now had to make a cool and calculated decision about the immediate future. Should he plump for the big bucks and join Abramovich's Russian revolution at Chelsea or should he remain at his beloved Liverpool? He had met with Anfield boss Rafael Benitez and, although he must have privately wished that his old mentor Gerard Houllier were still in charge, it was hard not be impressed by the amiable Spaniard. Benitez had, after all, shown the footballing super powers of Real Madrid and Barcelona how to win La Liga twice whilst with unfashionable Valencia, also taking the club to UEFA Cup glory. If he could achieve that level of success at Valencia, what might he achieve at Anfield?

Some Liverpool fans expressed their concerns when they heard that Steven Gerrard and Frank Lampard had become firm friends on and off the pitch for England and they knew that if Gerrard wanted to go, no one at Anfield could stop him. Liverpool chief executive Rick Parry told

the press, 'I hope that Rafael Benitez's appointment con-
vinces Steven that his future lies at Anfield. But you cannot
force anyone to stay against their wishes. He does not want
to get to thirty-five having been loyal to the club but found
he's never won a thing.' Anfield legend Ian Rush entered
the debate by declaring, 'It would be a big blow to lose a
player of his quality. He was by far the Reds' best player last
season. If Steven was to stay after all this transfer speculation,
it will be almost like signing a new big-name player.'

The press reported that Chelsea had made a £35 million bid for Gerrard, but Liverpool insisted they had not
received an approach from anyone for the player. Chelsea
TV broadcast an interview with their chief executive Peter
Kenyon in which he stated, 'Steven Gerrard is recognised
as one of the best midfielders around and were it possible
we would be extremely interested.'

Gerrard had recently signed a four-year contract at
Anfield but if he wanted to leave there was relatively little
they could do about it providing Chelsea – or another
suitor – came up with a large enough transfer fee. Jose
Mourinho, the newly installed Chelsea manager, said that
he would be delighted if Gerrard ended up at Stamford
Bridge: 'If he came here, I would welcome him with open
arms. If he doesn't come, I will still admire him as a player
and wish him all the best.'

The news that all Liverpool fans had been hoping to hear
came on 28 June. At an Anfield press conference Steven
Gerrard confirmed that he was staying at Liverpool. Gerrard
stated that he was relieved that all the speculation about his
future was over. He said, 'For the first time in my career, I
have really thought about the possibility of moving on to
a different club. The last month has really been confusing
for me. I've been involved in a big tournament, as you are
all aware. That's the reason why I have been really quiet
about my future. I haven't been really happy about the
progression of the club over the last two years, but I have

gone with a decision that is in my heart. I love the club. I love the supporters and that's what it boils down to at the end of the day.'

Gerrard's decision had been made after many hours discussing his future with his family, his friends, his girlfriend and his agent. The Liverpool star looked far from happy at the press conference as he told the football world of his decision to remain at Anfield. Football pundits took this as a sign that the saga of Gerrard's future at Liverpool had still not been laid to rest and would probably return in the not-too-distant future.

Rafael Benitez was thrilled to hear the news that Steven Gerrard was staying at the club. He, like most Reds fans, expected him to start the new season in the colours of Chelsea. Now he could plan for the new season with one of Euro 2004's best midfielders – as well as the tournament's star striker, Milan Baros – in his line-up. One of Gerard Houllier's parting gifts to Liverpool was the signature of French striker Djibril Cissé. Benitez also had world-class striker Michael Owen at his disposal for the time being, but his future at the club was also uncertain. Benitez had money to spend and other signings were certain to come to Anfield before the start of the new campaign.

As the Liverpool squad returned to Anfield after the summer break, many of them expressed their relief that Steven Gerrard would be starting the new season with them. Danny Murphy told the press, 'Normally Steven is very laid back and very easy going, but the last two weeks have been very difficult for him. I'm delighted he is staying. He is our captain and one of our most influential players. The fans relate to him because of his roots and his style of play. It's unusual in modern football for a player to make a decision not based on financial rewards, but that's the kind of lad he is.' Vladimir Smicer said, 'It's great news; we all know what Steven Gerrard means to Liverpool. I am happy and it's big news for the fans and the club for next season.'

One of Steven Gerrard's only demands after pledging his future to Liverpool was that he could wear the number 8 shirt for the new season. He did not give the reason for his request, but previous Anfield number 8s included Sammy Lee, John Aldridge, Brian Hall, Roger Hunt and Jimmy Case. Speculation among Reds' fans was that Jimmy Case was the closest to Gerrard in his dynamic style of play and that it was as a tribute to him that Steven Gerrard wanted to wear the same shirt.

Gerrard prepared for the new season happy that everything appeared to be in place for a title challenge. 'I wouldn't have stayed at the club if I didn't think we could win the Premiership,' declared the Liverpool midfielder on his first day back at Melwood. As for Rafael Benitez, Gerrard remarked, 'We've got a great manager and I'm looking forward to working with him. If we can win a trophy with him it would mean everything to me as Liverpool's captain.' As for the Champions League, Gerrard thought his team had a chance, 'I'm not saying we are going to win it, that would be unrealistic, although we would love to do it.'

One of the first problems Benitez faced in his early days as Liverpool's boss was making himself understood during team talks. 'Communicating is very hard. It will be difficult because the players still don't understand me. It will take at least three months before we can communicate properly,' said Benitez as Liverpool prepared for their first Premiership game of the season. As for the Liverpool accent, Benitez remarked, 'I can't understand it. It sounds Russian to me.'

Initial impressions of Rafael Benitez were that he was a polite, quiet type of person, similar in some ways to Gerard Houllier. He didn't appear to be the type of manager who would rant and rave at his players, but to have reached the top in Spain Benitez must have had a touch of steel about him. As the season progressed it also became more and more noticeable that his tactical awareness, particularly when it came to playing against European teams, was of the highest calibre. Perhaps Steven Gerrard's desire to lift the European Cup was not a pipe dream. Arsenal's Ashley Cole said that he was impressed with Liverpool's capture of Djibril Cissé and that the Anfield team and Chelsea would push them hard for their Premiership crown. 'Liverpool have bought really well in Cissé and the title race will be much tougher than last season. I think we'll have to be even better than last season,' declared Cole.

The Liverpool side that took on Spurs in the opening fixture of the 2004/05 season did not have Michael Owen or Danny Murphy in the line-up. As expected, Michael Owen had signed for Real Madrid, but the departure of Danny Murphy surprised many Liverpool fans. Murphy was snapped up by Charlton boss Alan Curbishley, who was delighted to take the tough midfielder to the London club. Benitez had brought in Spanish stars Luis Garcia, Antonio Nunez, Xabi Alonso and Josemi. He needed to recoup some money and Murphy was one of the players that he considered surplus to requirements. Danny Murphy is a strong-willed individual and there were suggestions that perhaps Benitez wanted to stamp his authority on his new team by moving on one of the more vociferous local lads in the squad. Whatever the reasons, Murphy was gone and some at Anfield were not happy, including his teammate Steven Gerrard.

Rafael Benitez was determined to stamp his mark on the club and from the outset he accomplished this. However, the notion that Benitez wanted his team full of Spanish imports led to fears that young local players would not receive their chance in the first team as had often happened in the past. Although Steven Gerrard was sad to see Murphy and Owen leave, he wished both of them the best of luck with their new clubs. On Michael Owen's departure Gerrard remarked, 'I have total respect for Michael and I respect his decision. He's been a great player for Liverpool and I wish him all the best.'

Liverpool drew their opening game against Spurs and did not make a particularly good start to their Premiership campaign, losing 3 of their opening 7 fixtures. In Europe, they scraped past Austria's AK Graz 2-1 on aggregate in a Champions League qualifier. The away leg was a personal triumph for Steven Gerrard, who scored both Liverpool goals.

Liverpool had made an inauspicious start under Benitez, but it was early days and the new boss seemed to be proving himself a popular figure with all at Anfield. Reserve team goalkeeper Paul Harrison told the Liverpool FC match-day programme that the new manager had impressed everyone, even the youth academy kids. The nineteen year old said, 'It's great to see the academy lads like Steven Warnock and Darren Potter getting a chance. Rafa doesn't have any favourites and it's all about the team. He has the right mentality and I like it. He talks and treats everyone the same. I think this is really encouraging for all the younger lads in particular.'

Even departing Reds star Michael Owen found time to express his confidence in Rafael Benitez getting things right at Anfield. Owen said, 'He's very good tactically and all the lads are enjoying working with him. With Rafael in charge and Steven Gerrard at the club, Liverpool are in safe hands. I get the impression that his first aim is to make the team very tight at the back. He'll work on the team after putting solid foundations in place.'

Rafael Benitez's attempts to improve his proficiency of the English language led to some hilarious moments on the training ground at Melwood. On one occasion he told a player to be careful about the wine when the opposition were taking free-kicks. The player scratched his head and said, 'Wine – do you mean wind?' Benitez laughed off his howler and told him that it was indeed the wind he meant and not the local wine.

To improve his English Benitez took to listening to his favourite band, the Beatles, as he drove to and from training sessions, his favourite tracks being 'Michelle' and 'Help'. It was early days for Rafael Benitez at Anfield, but in some ways there was something Shanklyesque about their new boss. Like the legendary Scot, he was one hundred per cent committed to the cause. He also had a sense of humour. Benitez liked nothing better than to spend time in the company of the Liverpool faithful having a chat and a beer. Shankly also spent a great deal of time passing the time of day chatting to football supporters, but being a teetotaller, he would do without the glass of beer.

Steven Gerrard took a break from the Benitez revolution at Anfield to join up with the England squad for two vital World Cup qualifiers against Austria and Poland in early September. Gerrard was a major doubt for the Austria game with a groin injury, but he passed a fitness test and scored his fifth goal for his country in a 2-2 draw. His groin held out for England's trip to Poland five days later and the side came away with a fine 2-1 victory. England and Steven Gerrard's dream of playing in a World Cup finals was still on track.

Liverpool then had to embark on a series of important fixtures from the end of September through to mid-November without their talismanic skipper. Gerrard sustained a broken metatarsal in Liverpool's 2-1 defeat against Manchester United on 20 September and did not recover full fitness for several weeks. During the period of Gerrard's absence Liverpool had a mixed bag of results in the Premiership and in Europe. Their chances of progressing in the Champions League hung by a thread after defeats against Monaco and Olympiakos in the group stages of the competition. Everyone at Anfield – indeed everyone in the country – knew how important Steven Gerrard's presence in the Liverpool team was. The player himself, however, interviewed while he was recovering from his broken foot, displayed noticeable modesty when asked about his absence from the team. Gerrard said, 'To be honest I don't think the team are missing me while I am out. They've got Xabi Alonso playing well and for me he's one of the best midfielders in the world. There's also Didi Hamann who I rate very highly. To be honest there's not much I can do anyway at the moment apart from sit on the couch with my foot in the air. We've made progress this season and we've got to keep pushing on.'

Steven Gerrard returned to the Liverpool team for the visit to Middlesbrough in November, a game that the Reds lost 2-0. They then lost to Monaco 1-0 in the Champions League, but recovered their form with a fine 2-1 victory over Arsenal the following week. The crunch game in their pursuit of a place in the Champions League knock-out stages came against Olympiakos on 8 December at Anfield. Liverpool needed to beat the Greek team to progress in the competition but Olympiakos, with the brilliant Rivaldo in their line-up, were tough opposition. Rivaldo's best years in football were now behind him, but when he scored directly from a free-kick to give Olympiakos the lead, he looked again like the Brazilian star who had thrilled football fans throughout the world with his incredible skills.

The Reds were up against it. A draw would put Olympiakos through and Liverpool didn't look capable of breaching the Greeks' defence twice. Goals from Florent Sinama-Pongolle and Neil Mellor then put Liverpool in the driving seat. Inspired by Rivaldo, Olympiakos refused to give up and pushed forward for an equaliser. With the tension inside Anfield almost at fever pitch, Steven Gerrard then produced a moment of superb footballing skill. He was fully twenty-five yards from the Olympiakos goal when he let fly with a tremendous strike that flew past their goalkeeper before he had time to react. The game was won and Liverpool had gained a place in the knock-out stages of the Champions League. The Liverpool fans erupted in homage to their hero Steven Gerrard. Liverpool legend Kenny Dalglish was a spectator at the game and described

118

Gerrard's goal as one of the greatest that he had ever seen. 'From the moment that the ball left his boot you were sure it was going to trouble the Olympiakos goalkeeper,' said Dalglish, 'but the swerve and cut that Gerrard put on the ball meant that their 'keeper was never going to get close to it. It was a stunning goal.' Next in line for Liverpool in the Champions League were Bayer Leverkusen. The German side had topped their group, which contained Real Madrid, Roma and Dynamo Kiev, to win through to the knock-out stage and were expected to provide a stern test for Liverpool.

As the new year began, Chelsea, the team that Steven Gerrard had turned down in the summer, appeared to be strong favourites to win their first ever Premiership title. In fact, many soccer pundits believed that they were capable of winning every competition that they were competing in that season. Liverpool lagged well behind them in the Premiership but, after beating Watford in the Carling Cup semi-finals, the Reds had an opportunity to deprive the Stamford Bridge team of one of those trophies.

Apart from their success against Watford, the new year did not begin too well for Liverpool. Burnley knocked them out of the FA Cup in the third round and the Reds fell further behind in the Premiership when Manchester United came to Anfield and won 1-0 through a Wayne Rooney goal. Spanish international Fernando Morientes was brought in by Rafael Benitez to help boost Liverpool's goalscoring tally, but he was unavailable for Champions League games.

Liverpool defied the predictions of the majority of soccer pundits by fighting their way through to the Champions League quarter-finals. Stunning victories over Deportivo, Olympiakos and Bayer Leverkusen on their way to the last eight of the competition suddenly had the rest of Europe sitting up and taking notice of Benitez's team. They may have been underachievers in the Premiership, but in Europe

119

they looked a different outfit. Benitez knew how to win in Europe and, although Liverpool were underdogs for their quarter-final tie against Italian giants Juventus, the Reds boss was confident of reaching the semis.

Liverpool against Juventus at Anfield on 5 April 2005 was one of those great European nights that the Reds have been famous for over the years. The Italians were packed with world-class players in their line-up, such as Pavel Nedved, Alessandro Del Piero, Gianluigi Buffon, David Trezeguet and Lillian Thuram. The roar that greeted them as they ran out to face Liverpool at Anfield on that April evening would have put the fear of God into even the most experienced players. Liverpool hit them with everything in the first half as the Kop roared them on from the very first minute of the game. Juventus looked shell-shocked and it was no surprise when Sami Hyypia put the Reds into the lead. Garcia added another and Liverpool could have gone in four up at half-time. 'Given the calibre of opposition, that was the best performance I can ever remember during all my time at Anfield,' Steven Gerrard said after the game when asked about the Reds' first-half display against Juventus.

The Italians were gifted a lifeline in the second half when Liverpool's stand-in goalkeeper Scott Carson made a costly mistake that allowed Fabio Cannavaro to pull a goal back. The game finished 2-1 and Juventus were now back in the tie.

Liverpool went to Turin needing at least a draw to be certain of going through to the semi-finals. Steven Gerrard was optimistic that the Reds would do it. 'We've beaten one of the best teams in Europe and not many people would have given us a chance,' he said. 'We know how difficult it will be in Turin, so a lot of us are going to have to put in the best performances of our careers. There's a semi-final place for us if we can put in another performance like that.'

As it turned out, Juventus appeared to be still in a state of shock from the first leg. The Italians seemed strangely lethargic in the second leg and Liverpool produced a solid defensive display with very few scares to book their place against Chelsea in the semi-finals. Many scratched their heads in disbelief; had Liverpool really just seen off the mighty Juventus to obtain a Champions League semi-final spot? They were now just three games away from winning the European Cup. Judging by their Premiership form it didn't seem possible, but in Europe Rafael Benitez certainly had the magic touch.

At the end of March England took on Northern Ireland in a World Cup qualifier. Eriksson's team comfortably won the game 4-0, strikes from Joe Cole, Michael Owen, Frank Lampard and a Chris Baird own goal securing the points. England now had a strong grip on their qualifying group and a 2-0 victory against Azerbaijan four days later confirmed them as strong favourites to reach the 2006 World Cup finals. Steven Gerrard was employed by Sven-Goran Eriksson in a deeper midfield role to allow Frank Lampard to make his probing attacking runs. The debate over just where Gerrard's best position was for his country continued to grow throughout 2005. Like Lampard, Gerrard could also play the more attacking role but, as he had mentioned in many interviews, the Liverpool midfielder was happy to play in any position for England so long as he was in the team.

Once again Gerrard's stint with the England squad sparked more rumours in the press that the Liverpool captain was about to join Jose Mourinho's Chelsea team. It was a story that was destined to run and run throughout the summer. Gerrard's goal against Azerbaijan was his sixth for this country. It was obvious that if he was employed in a more attacking role by Eriksson he would probably soon become acclaimed as one of the best attacking midfielders in world football. His goals tally for Liverpool throughout 2005 made impressive reading. Frank Lampard was, however, in a rich vein of form for club and country and his goalscoring record would have made impressive reading for an out-and-out striker, never mind a midfield player. For the time being Lampard had made the attacking midfield role in the England side his own. Sven-Goran Eriksson had a dilemma: where to play two world-class attacking midfielders in his team? David Beckham looked secure in the England line-up for the foreseeable future. One thing, however, did look certain: injury permitting, Gerrard would be a permanent feature of the England side for many years to come.

In the final of the Carling Cup, extra-time goals from Didier Drogba and Mateja Kezman ensured that Liverpool went home from Cardiff empty-handed. An early strike by John Arne Riise was cancelled out by an unfortunate Steven Gerrard own goal and thereafter the scores remained level until the end of normal time. Antonio Nunez made it 3-2 near the end but Chelsea held out to take the cup. People across the country joked about Gerrard's aberration as 'his first goal for Chelsea' – as if there were many more to come. Clearly, many observers felt that the midfielder's rumoured summer move to the Blues was already a done deal.

In the Premiership, Liverpool were involved in a titanic struggle with Everton and Bolton for the fourth Champions League spot. Everton had been the surprise package of the season and, although their form had dipped recently, they were fighting tooth and nail to hang on to fourth position in the table. At the heart of Liverpool's inconsistent Premiership form was their inability to score goals away from home. They had once again become afflicted by the Jekyll and Hyde syndrome that had dogged Gerard Houllier's reign at the club. They couldn't take the points against the Premiership's lesser teams, yet regularly turned the elite over.

In the Champions League, however, it was a totally different matter. Rafael Benitez was proving to be a master tactician in Europe. Benitez had won the UEFA Cup the previous season with Valencia and, although Liverpool were the Champions League outsiders with the bookies, his team had developed a habit of defying the odds.

Liverpool's Champions League semi-final against Chelsea produced two titanic encounters. The Reds went to Stamford Bridge for the first leg and held them to a 0-0 draw. Chelsea boss Jose Mourinho told the press that he wasn't particularly concerned by the draw and that he was confident of reaching the final by getting a good result at Anfield. Steven Gerrard was equally confident that his team would be competing in the final at the Ataturk Olympic Stadium in Istanbul on the 25 May. Gerrard said, 'We know now that we are just one win away from the final. We'll have the backing of the fans at Anfield and that should act as a spur. I really think that the fans could prove to be a vital factor.' Liverpool boss Rafael Benitez said before the home leg against Chelsea, 'With Steven Gerrard there is a sense of destiny. It's his dream to play for Liverpool in a Champions League final. For me Steve will be a key player. He looks forward to important games like this. We respect Chelsea and their achievement in winning the Premiership, but I don't say we can win, I say we will win.'

Steven Gerrard spoke about the impact that the fans would have on the game against Chelsea and the roar that greeted the two teams as they ran out at Anfield must have instilled a sense of fear and trepidation in even the most experienced campaigners in the Chelsea side. The Liverpool fans had roared their team to victory over Juventus a month earlier in the Champions League and against Chelsea the atmosphere they created was sensational. Many commentators had suggested that if Chelsea had had a following like the Reds then the Premiership champions would already have a foothold in the final. Chelsea skipper John Terry said that as the two teams waited to run out at Anfield Jose Mourinho had told the Blues to forget about the atmosphere. This, however, proved impossible, as Terry recalled:

'The Liverpool fans that night were amazing. The hairs on my arms were standing up. I just kept looking around, trying to take it all in. I wasn't daunted by it, but it was amazing. There's no point denying there's a special atmosphere there. A lot of other grounds seem to have lost it. I wish there were more crowds like that.'

John Terry and his team faced a crowd and a team on fire. Roared on by their supporters, Steven Gerrard led the charge and after only four minutes Liverpool took a controversial lead. The Chelsea players were certain that Garcia's lob had been cleared without the ball crossing the goal-line. The referee allowed the goal to stand and Anfield erupted. Chelsea had enough chances in the rest of the game to have clawed back Liverpool's lead, but the Reds, inspired by Steven Gerrard and the equally outstanding Jamie Carragher, held on for one of the most famous victories in the club's history. They had won through to the Champions League final against all the odds and the predictions of the so-called football experts. They would take on one of the most outstanding teams in Europe in the final, AC Milan, the champions of Italy.

Liverpool prepared for their date with destiny against AC Milan on 25 May, in the knowledge that they had failed in their bid to finish fourth in the Premiership. If they didn't beat Milan in the final there would be no Champions League football for Liverpool the following season. This would have hit the club severely financially and Rafael Benitez's first season in charge, despite reaching one minor and one major final, would have been deemed a relative failure. They had finished a distance behind Chelsea in the Premiership and even local rivals Everton had, somewhat unexpectedly, finished above them in the table, a state of affairs that had been unheard of on Merseyside for years. Some said that going into the final as major underdogs would mean that the Reds had little pressure on them when they took the field on that warm Istanbul evening.

Steven Gerrard told the press that he was desperate to win the Champions League for the fans: 'To come back empty-handed from Istanbul would be a disaster. We need to make sure we bring the cup home. We will dedicate it to the fans because they have waited a long time for that success. In Europe we have shown we will die for the shirt.' Gerrard revealed that since Liverpool had knocked out Chelsea he had thought of nothing else but the final. 'Since we beat Chelsea I have been dreaming about it,' he said. 'I would like nothing better than to score in the final.'

An estimated 20,000 Liverpool fans with tickets, and thousands more without, flew to Turkey for the game. In Liverpool city centre huge television screens relayed the game to those who didn't make the trip. Even the management at Liverpool's grand Philharmonic Hall decided to broadcast their first ever football match.

If Steven Gerrard was now the King of the Kop, Jamie Carragher ran him a close second in the popularity stakes at Anfield. Carragher had been a revelation throughout the season. If it wasn't for the fact that the England team was particularly well off for central defenders he would have won many more caps for his country. Carragher, like Steven Gerrard, was about to play in the biggest game of his career. He told the *Liverpool Echo*, 'There were times during this season when I thought we were a million miles from winning the Champions League. This shows you can never be sure of anything in football. It seems like every Liverpool supporter I know has come here. We want to take the trophy back to Merseyside for them.'

Steven Gerrard had said that if Liverpool won the cup then he would take it on a tour of Huyton, the place where his friends and family still lived. Carragher was told about his teammate's plans and joked, 'I won't be taking the trophy to any alehouses in Bootle, where I come from, if we win it. There are too many Evertonian friends of mine around there. I wouldn't want any of them near it.'

Liverpool at the start of their Champions League campaign were 100/1 to win the trophy. Before the game these odds had tumbled to 7/4, but they were still regarded as rank outsiders against an outstanding AC Milan team. By half-time the Reds were once again available at massively long odds after the Italians had produced one of the most sensational forty-five minutes of football that anyone had seen in years. Liverpool were 3-0 down, Milan were on a different planet and the only question being posed by football pundits was how many the Italians would win by?

The Reds fans in the stadium and back home on Merseyside were shell-shocked. It was estimated that 45,000 Liverpool fans were packed into the stadium, outnumbering the Milan supporters by at least two to one. Although they were crestfallen after their team's first-half trouncing, some of them began to sing the Liverpool anthem 'You'll Never Walk Alone'. Thousands more began to join in and the dejected Liverpool team, slumped in their dressing room heard the singing. Rafael Benitez was in the process of telling his side not to let their heads drop. 'We are Liverpool. You are playing for Liverpool. Don't forget that,' he drummed into them. Sounding not unlike the great Bill Shankly must have when he needed to come up with something quick to inspire a badly shaken team. Benitez told them, 'Listen to that singing. You cannot call yourselves Liverpool players if you have your heads down. You have to hold your heads high for the supporters. You have to do it for them.'

Midfielder Luis Garcia said he couldn't believe it when he heard the singing: 'We were sitting in the dressing room and could clearly hear thousands of fans singing "You'll Never Walk Alone". Can you imagine how that felt? We were 3-0 down and all we could hear was 45,000 people letting us know they still believed in us. It was at that point that we started to believe too.'

Rafael Benitez made a few tactical changes, bringing on Dietmar Hamann in an attempt to stop the brilliant Kaka and Pirlo from dominating the midfield. Benitez sent them out for the second half with the words 'Give yourselves the chance to be heroes. Believe you can do it and we will do it.'

AC Milan almost went four goals up at the beginning of the second half. Liverpool needed something special to galvanise them into action. It came, almost inevitably, from their captain Steven Gerrard. Gerrard said before the game that he had dreamt about scoring against Milan. In the fifty-fourth minute, when he rose to head Riise's cross past Dida, his dream had come true. Gerrard was now a totally different player to the one in the first half who had laboured against the classy Italians. He ran back to the centre-circle after the goal waving his arms at the Liverpool fans to implore them to keep going with their inspiring support for the team.

Liverpool now began to play like a team possessed and Steven Gerrard was at the heart of their attempt to drag themselves back into the game. After fifty-six minutes Smicer hit a low drive that beat the Milan goalkeeper to nestle in the bottom corner of the net. AC Milan might have been a brilliant team but if they were put under pressure they were prone to crumbling, just as they had a year earlier in the 2003/04 season when Deportivo scored four against them to knock them out of the Champions League.

The Liverpool fans in the stadium and back home in the city centre were now dancing a jig of joy as they watched their team come back from the dead to give themselves a chance of getting something from the game. Just three minutes later the comeback was completed when Steven Gerrard surged into the Milan penalty area only to be brought down by Gennaro Gattuso's challenge. Dida in the Milan goal saved Xabi Alonso's penalty but the quick-thinking Spaniard followed up to put the rebound in the net. In a fantastic five-minute spell Liverpool had scored three goals. This was the stuff of dreams. AC Milan were in a trance, their supporters in the stadium feeling the same as their heroes on the pitch. This was not supposed to happen and they could barely believe it. The final half-hour of the game fell back into a more normal pattern of play with both teams apparently happy to let the game go into extra time or even penalties. This had been a sensational game and both teams were reluctant to leave the field as losers. Milan had been brilliant in the first half, Liverpool sensational in the second.

Milan almost won the game during extra time but Dudek in the Liverpool goal pulled off a fantastic double save to keep the Italians out. The dreaded penalty shootout saw Jerzy Dudek become the hero of Liverpool when he employed a variety of unconventional goalkeeping tactics, reminiscent of Bruce Grobbelaar, to save three spot-kicks and win the trophy for the Reds. The Liverpool supporters in Istanbul went crazy, as did the millions of Reds fans across the globe as they celebrated the most sensational fightback in European Cup history.

Prime Minister Tony Blair sent a telegram to the team stating, 'Unbelievable, incredible, brilliant. The whole country is proud of you.' Liverpool hero Jamie Carragher had played his heart out for his team and after the game he said, 'Our manager can stand up at press conferences next season and say "I am a European champion" – Jose Mourinho can't say that anymore.' Steven Gerrard had been inspirational in Liverpool's fightback and in the second half had almost single-handedly dragged his team back into the match. If he was Liverpool's most popular modern-day hero before the final, he was now on his way to joining the all-time Anfield legends. Before the game he was still constantly being quizzed about his future by the press. The constant probing about where he would be plying his trade in the coming season now appeared to be at an end when, punchdrunk with joy, he said after the final, 'How can I leave Liverpool after a night like this?' Liverpool fans, however, were still not totally convinced and another summer of 'will he go or will he stay?' appeared to be on the horizon yet again.

eleven

The Heart and Soul of Liverpool

Steven Gerrard settled down for the summer break still on a high after Liverpool's stunning Champions League success. Back home at his luxury Blundellsands home near Southport, he relived the final over and over again. 'He never shut up about it. He kept saying "I can't believe it",' his fiancée Alex Curran told the *Daily Mirror* when they asked about his reaction to what had happened in Istanbul.

As he had throughout the season, Steven Gerrard spent most of the summer of 2005 fending off questions about his proposed move to Chelsea, Real Madrid, Barcelona or whichever club had the money to buy him. Speculation increased that Chelsea would finally get their man and a world-record £50 million fee was mentioned in many newspapers. To escape the pressure he went on a golfing holiday to the Algarve. Gerrard's favourite sportsman is Tiger Woods and if he hadn't become an outstanding footballer he might have taken up golf.

When Steven Gerrard arrived home he still hadn't made up his mind. The suspense went on throughout June for his legion of admirers. Then, in early July, it appeared that Gerrard was about to sign for Chelsea. A press conference was expected to be announced and the general consensus was that the Liverpool midfielder would be moving to the London club on 5 July. Liverpool fans were dismayed and many were angry. After the Champions League victory in May, Gerrard had said that there was no way that he could leave the Reds. What had happened since to change his mind? They waited for the devastating news to be confirmed. But then one of the most dramatic U-turns in the history of British football was relayed to disbelieving Reds fans. Steven Gerrard had decided that he wanted to remain at Anfield after all and would soon be signing a new contract that would keep him at the club until 2009. Liverpool fans, when they got over the shock, were elated. The greatest Anfield idol since the days of Dalglish had pledged his future to Liverpool.

Steven Gerrard had embarrassed himself by his indecision and had even told Rafael Benitez to strip him of the captaincy of the club. 'It's been the hardest six weeks of my life because I wrongly believed the club didn't want me,' Gerrard told the *Liverpool Echo*. Club chairman David Moores said, 'Steven changed his mind because he knew what he'd miss if he went elsewhere. He was confused and we'd rather have done without it, but it will never happen again. We have kept our captain and it means a hell of a lot to me.'

Rafael Benitez rejected Gerrard's offer to give up the Liverpool captaincy after discussing the matter with some of his other players. Gerrard also explained what had happened to his Liverpool teammates, who had become as dismayed by all the rumours as the Reds' supporters were. When the dust had settled, everyone at Anfield was happy with Gerrard's decision. The Liverpool star's new contract was reported to have been worth around the £100,000-a-week mark, probably less than what Chelsea had offered him, but whatever the true figure was only Gerrard, his agent and Liverpool Football Club will ever know. 'I've committed my long-term future to the club and I want all the speculation to end now. This is all I wanted all along,' said Gerrard. 'It's a weight off my mind and I just want to put this mess behind us. I've only one medal left to win at Liverpool and that's the Premiership. Liverpool is the only place I've ever wanted to win it.'

Gerrard concluded his press statement with the following words: 'In my heart, this is my club. I never want to go through this again. I've been at this club since I was eight. I've got a great relationship with people here. I just feel the club deserve the next five to ten years of my career and I don't want to give those years to any other club. I want to give them to Liverpool.'

Rafael Benitez, like all the Liverpool supporters, was delighted that Steven Gerrard had pledged his future to the club. The season for Liverpool was destined to start early with Champions League qualifiers having to be played before the Reds could play in the group stages of the competition. There had been concerns all summer that Liverpool might not even be allowed by UEFA to compete in the Champions League after they finished out of the top four in the Premiership. UEFA relented and allowed the European champions to defend their crown. Steven Gerrard considered that his team had been fortunate to be allowed into the competition and said, 'We are lucky to be here and counting our blessings. Rules are rules and we didn't qualify, it was as simple as that. If we had finished above Everton we would have avoided all this, so it's our own fault.'

Although Liverpool's opening qualifying games were against complete European minnows, Steven Gerrard was in blistering goalscoring form, knocking in five against Welsh side TNS over the two legs and two against Lithuanian champions Kaunas. Liverpool's record goalscorer in Europe was Michael Owen with 22 goals, so the fact that Gerrard was already on a tally of 15 was pretty sensational for a midfield player. He made it 16 after coming on in the final stages of the second leg against Kaunas; Michael Owen's record appeared to be well within his range. Liverpool then progressed to the Champions League group stages by knocking out Bulgarian side CSKA Sofia in their final qualifying game. A strong challenge to retain their Champions League crown was now expected from Benitez's team.

Rafael Benitez actually began planning for the 2005/06 season the day after Liverpool's Champions League success over AC Milan. He told journalist Martin Samuel, 'After the match I said to my staff that we now need to make decisions and that is my responsibility. In football if you talk only of memories you will never win the next game.' Players that had featured in Liverpool's Champions League campaign, such as Smicer, Baros, Biscan and Nunez, were shipped out. Promising midfielder Momo Sissoko and giant striker Peter Crouch, along with Holland's left-sided midfielder Bolo Zenden, were signed by Benitez to strengthen the Liverpool squad.

At the start of the Premiership season Liverpool carried on where they had left off the previous campaign by looking distinctly average. Chelsea came to Anfield early in October and came away with a 4-1 victory. Steven Gerrard smashed in the Reds' only goal, but it must have crossed his mind that if it hadn't been for his deep affection for the Anfield outfit he would probably now have been playing in the blue of Chelsea.

In Europe it was a different matter, Liverpool comfortably reached the group stages of the Champions League. They were pitted against Real Betis, Anderlecht and archrivals Chelsea but had few problems in reaching the knockout stages of the competition. They even took time out to win the European Super Cup, beating CSKA Moscow in the one-off game played in Monaco. Local hero Jamie

Carragher had the honour of captaining Liverpool to this victory, Steven Gerrard missing the game through injury.

Gerrard travelled to Monaco with the Liverpool squad to receive a UEFA award when he was named Europe's most valuable player. The Liverpool midfielder received further accolades for his outstanding footballing talent when he was named as BBC North West's Footballer of the Year with the Reds winning the Team of the Year award. In Europe, Steven Gerrard finished in third place behind the winner Ronaldinho and runner-up Frank Lampard in the Ballon d'Or prize for the European Footballer of the Year. The brilliant Brazilian, Ronaldinho, said of the two English midfield stars, Lampard and Gerrard, 'They are both players with a lot of quality. Lampard and Gerrard are great players and they deserve to be rewarded in this way. It gives me a great deal of pleasure to see them play in the Premiership. It is great to see such talented young footballers.' The voting in the Ballon d'Or was Ronaldinho 225 votes, Lampard 148 and Gerrard 142.

Steven Gerrard might have now been recognised throughout Europe as an outstanding player, but his early-season form was a cause of concern to him. England had some vital World Cup qualifying games to contend with in September and October. A warm-up game in Denmark in mid-August went disastrously wrong for Sven-Goran Eriksson's team when they were thrashed 4-1. The knives were now out for the Swede and when England scrapped a 1-0 victory over Wales and then fell to an incredible 1-0 defeat to Northern Ireland in Belfast in World Cup quali-fying games, the team came under tremendous pressure. Coming up were much tougher opposition in the shape of Austria and Poland. Victory over Austria was necessary to make qualification for the 2006 World Cup finals, to be held in Germany, absolutely certain. Frank Lampard held his nerve to score the only goal of the game from the penalty spot after Michael Owen was fouled in the box.

Despite the at times bitter press campaign against Eriksson and his managerial style, England were through to the World Cup finals. Steven Gerrard was injured and missed the game against Poland, which England won 2-1, but the match now had no meaning attached to it, Eriksson's team having already qualified for Germany.

Everyone in the England camp was delighted to have reached the World Cup finals, none more so than Steven Gerrard, who had had to sit at home for the 2002 World Cup after injury put him out of the tournament. The midfielder's performances in the defeats against Northern Ireland and Denmark, and his early-season form in general, had not reached the extremely high standards that Steven Gerrard set himself. 'The Northern Ireland game was the lowest point I've had with England,' he remarked. 'The 4-1 defeat against Denmark wasn't good either, but it was only a friendly. My performances of late for England have been very average so I need to raise my game.'

As for his partnership in midfield with Frank Lampard, Gerrard said, 'The partnership with Frank can definitely improve as I don't think that we've set the world alight. Naturally, I'm a bit more defensive than Frank and maybe he likes to break forward more than me. What Sven wants is that if one of us breaks forward, the other one will be disciplined and stay back. I've spoken to Frank about it a lot and we'll work on it.'

Just which is Steven Gerrard's best position for his country will probably be a national debate with football fans until the 2006 World Cup finals actually begin. Sven-Goran Eriksson is confident that Gerrard is happy to play in a variety of roles for his country and is equally adept at whatever position he is asked to play. In England's final game of 2005, the friendly against Argentina which Eriksson's team won 3-2, Gerrard played in three roles during the match. He started on the left of midfield and was then switched to a more central role and ended the game wide on the right. His fantastic cross from the right wing for one of Michael Owen's goals in the game against Argentina was reminiscent of David Beckham's crossing ability at its best. Sven-Goran Eriksson said that Steven Gerrard was flexible enough to play in a variety of positions for his country: 'Steven doesn't have any problems with playing in different roles. It works for Liverpool, sometimes even in the same game. He can play second striker, wide left, wide right or where he is needed and that makes him a complete player. Steven says he is happy wherever he plays and he is a player who always knows what he has to do on the pitch, even if he hasn't been told.'

Liverpool's uninspiring start to the Premiership campaign had some soccer pundits expressing doubts about Rafael Benitez's ability to improve on what the last incumbent of the job, Gerard Houllier, had achieved at Liverpool. To have won the European Cup in his first season at the club was a fantastic achievement but in the English game the Reds were underachievers. Success in Europe had glossed over Liverpool's Premiership failings and their indifferent start to the 2005/06 season had many expressing concern that Benitez would ever be a success in English football.

In Europe he had proved himself a master tactician. There was even talk that he would take over at Real Madrid before the season was over. Benitez was born in Madrid and the brilliant form of their arch-rivals, Barcelona, had exposed them as a team that might be looking for a new man at the helm before too long. Benitez himself dismissed the Madrid speculation out of hand and said that his rebuilding Liverpool as a Premiership force had only just begun.

Defeat at Crystal Palace in the Carling Cup put renewed pressure on Rafael Benitez, but Steven Gerrard sprang to his manager's defence. Gerrard said, 'The performance at Palace was just not acceptable. A lot of our fans had paid good money to see that and what they saw wasn't good enough for Liverpool Football Club. But I don't see why anyone should blame Rafael Benitez. He's been saying the right things to us and doing the right things. It's the players who have to take the blame not the manager.' Benitez himself had just been named as the best manager in Europe in a poll conducted in Italy that put him ahead of successful Italian coaches Fabio Capello and Carlo Ancelotti.

The defeat at Crystal Palace proved something of a watershed for Liverpool as 2005 moved into its final months. Benitez demanded a change of attitude from his players. He said, 'We know we need to change our attitude, particularly after European games.' The Palace boss, Iain Dowie, told the press, 'European football is more ponderous and slower than the Premiership. It gives players more time on the ball and that's why Liverpool have done better in Europe, but I would be amazed if Liverpool are not in the top four come the end of the season.'

Iain Dowie's prediction that Liverpool would be in the top four in the Premiership by the end of the season had many doubting his powers of prediction. By the beginning of December, however, Liverpool's Premiership form had improved to such an extent that their 3-0 victory over the Premiership surprise package, Wigan, saw them move up to second spot in the table. Rafael Benitez's rebuilding of Liverpool was from the start based on a rock solid defence and the Reds, apart from their 4-1 nightmare against Chelsea at Anfield, had become a team that leaked very few goals. There was now little talk of Benitez leaving Anfield for pastures new as the Reds finally began to look one of the most solid outfits in the Premiership. Whether they will catch up with Chelsea in their pursuit of their first ever Premiership title is still open to debate. Jamie Carragher recently remarked, 'I feel that we are still behind Chelsea in terms of quality.' The fact that Liverpool ended the 2005/06 season in third spot, just one point behind Manchester United and nine behind Premiership Champions Chelsea, bodes well for the future.

For Steven Gerrard, 2006 could be a momentous year. The player, who has been acclaimed as one of the finest midfielders in world football, has now become the shining star of the Liverpool team. With Benitez as manager and Gerrard the driving force on the pitch, the Reds now have their best chance of building a title-winning team since the days when Kenny Dalglish was running the team.

In the summer of 2006, injury permitting, Steven Gerrard will play in a World Cup finals for the first time in his career. Although Brazil have an outstanding chance of retaining the trophy, Sven-Goran Eriksson's talented young squad also have the capacity to bring the World Cup back to the home of football for the first time since 1966.

Steven Gerrard has already signed a contract that hopefully will keep him at Anfield for many years to come. Current manager Rafael Benitez has publicly stated that when his term as Liverpool boss comes to an end he would like to see Steven Gerrard take over the reins from him. For the twenty-five-year-old Gerrard, that day is a long way off. Steven Gerrard as Liverpool manager is not, however, an idle dream. He recently stated, 'It's always been my idea to stay at Liverpool for as long as I can. Whether it's in a managerial or coaching capacity I'm not sure.' Steven Gerrard's words will no doubt make his legions of fans around the globe extremely happy indeed. For there is little doubt that Steven Gerrard is the modern-day heart and soul of a worldwide institution known as Liverpool Football Club.

Stevie G's Golden Moments

Tottenham Hotspur 2 Liverpool 1
Premiership, White Hart Lane, 5 December 1998

This was Steven Gerrard's full debut for Liverpool in the Premiership. Spurs provided the opposition and, despite the fact that all three goals came from the bodies of the men wearing red, Liverpool lost 2-1.

The first came when a Ruel Fox shot was deflected past David James in the Liverpool goal by one of his own defenders for the opener. Jamie Carragher then kicked the ball into his own net to put his side two goals down just after half-time. Despite Patrik Berger putting Liverpool back into the match with a fantastic strike from a free-kick in the fifty-fifth minute, the Reds lost 2-1. Steven Gerrard's first game had ended in defeat. David Thompson came on for Gerrard near the end, but the Liverpool youngster had impressed on his debut.

Gerrard had been given a brief taste of Premiership action when he came on in the eighty-ninth minute for Vegard Heggem in the Anfield game against Blackburn

Rovers on 29 November. Liverpool won that game 2-0 with goals from Ince and Owen.

Experienced Premiership campaigner Paul Ince was certainly impressed with young Steven Gerrard's debut. 'He acquitted himself very well with some nice touches. He's definitely one for the future,' concluded Ince.

Tottenham Hotspur: Walker, Carr, Young, Campbell, Sinton, Fox, Anderton, Nielsen, Ginola, Iversen, Ferdinand (32), Armstrong.

Liverpool: James, Babb, Staunton, Carragher, Heggem, Gerrard (Thompson 72), Ince, Berger, Bjornebye (Murphy 75), Owen, Fowler.

Liverpool 0 Celta Vigo 1
UEFA Cup third round, Anfield, 8 December 1998

Steven Gerrard's full Anfield debut was in this UEFA Cup defeat against Spanish club Celta Vigo. Liverpool had lost the away leg 3-1 with Gerrard sitting on the bench.

Although his first experience of a European night at Anfield was destined to end in defeat it was still a thrilling experience for the youngster from Huyton to be playing on such a stage. Gerard Houllier was confident that Steven Gerrard could handle playing in such a vital game and the young midfielder let no one down.

Celta Vigo had knocked out Aston Villa in the previous round and were a talented outfit. Gerrard played in place of the injured Jamie Redknapp and the Anfield crowd were particularly impressed by the youngster's ability to play inch-perfect through balls.

Unfortunately the Liverpool strike force of Michael Owen, Robbie Fowler and Karlheinz Riedle failed to capitalise on some good opportunities. Celta Vigo's goal came in the fifty-eighth minute when Makelele, who would later go on to achieve fame and fortune with Real Madrid and Chelsea, fed Revivo with a superb pass. Revivo skimmed past Gerrard and Murphy to make the tie safe by shooting past James in the Liverpool goal.

'Congratulations to Celta Vigo,' said Liverpool boss Gerard Houllier after the game. 'They were the best team on the night.'

Liverpool: James (Friedel 62 mins), McAteer, Carragher, Babb (Murphy 46), Matteo, Staunton, Gerrard, Thompson (Riedle 59), Berger, Fowler, Owen.
Celta Vigo: Dutruel, Salgado, Caceras, Djorovic, Berges, Karpin, Mazinho (Caires 86), Makelele, Mostovoi, Sanchez (Gudelj 76), Revivo (Tomas 70).

Liverpool 4 Sheffield Wednesday 1
Premiership, Anfield, 5 December 1999

Steven Gerrard scored his first senior goal for Liverpool in this Premiership encounter. This victory took the Reds up to fifth place in the table and some soccer pundits suggested that Houllier's team might be good enough to challenge for the title. Liverpool's outstanding players were local lads David Thompson, Danny Murphy and Steven Gerrard. Murphy and Gerrard were destined to achieve full England recognition. Gerrard was still only nineteen years old and scoring his first goal for the Reds was a dream come true.

Sheffield Wednesday opened the scoring with a brilliant strike from Niclas Alexandersson on twenty minutes. Sami Hyypia then brought Liverpool level, heading home a Thompson corner. Just before half-time Danny Murphy put the Reds into the lead when he volleyed past Pressman in the Wednesday goal. Steven Gerrard's golden moment came next when he put Liverpool 3-1 in front. The Liverpool midfielder scored after seventy minutes when he swept past three Sheffield Wednesday defenders and blasted the ball home. David Thompson wrapped up proceedings when he skipped past Briscoe and shot into the bottom corner.

Steven Gerrard's memories of his first Liverpool goal were, 'I picked up the ball outside their area, went past a few defenders and was determined to make good contact and at least hit the target. I was delighted when I saw the ball hit the back of the net.'

Liverpool: Westerveld, Song (Carragher 72), Henchoz, Hyypia, Matteo, Thompson, Hamann, Gerrard, Murphy (Staunton 76), Owen (Fowler 80), Camara.
Sheffield Wednesday: Pressman, Nolan, Thome, Walker, Briscoe (Sibon 80), Alexandersson, Atherton, Jonk, Rudi (Quinn 89), De Bilde (Cresswell 78), Booth.

England Under-21s 3 Yugoslavia Under-21s 0
Qualifier for Euro 2000 Under-21 Finals, Barcelona,
30 March 2000

This was the game that clinched Steven Gerrard's place in Kevin Keegan's full England squad. Gerrard was sensational playing in a holding role in front of an England back three of Gareth Barry, Rio Ferdinand and Jamie Carragher. Throughout the game Gerrard sprayed inch-perfect passes to Emile Heskey and Andy Campbell up front.

Campbell opened the scoring after twenty-four minutes following Gerrard's quickly taken free-kick when Heskey crossed for Campbell to slot home. The England captain, West Ham's Frank Lampard, then scored with a spot-kick to make the score 2-0. Steven Gerrard was then involved in the move of the match in the sixty-third minute when he found Seth Johnson with a fantastic crossfield pass. Johnson then passed to Lee Hendrie, who cleverly eluded a Yugoslavian defender before slipping the ball past the goalkeeper to make it 3-0.

England had star performers all over the pitch, Rio Ferdinand, Frank Lampard and Emile Heskey all boosting their chances of gaining a place in Keegan's Euro 2000 squad. Steven Gerrard, however, was the night's greatest star and looked a certainty to play for the full England team soon.

England Under-21s: Wright, Dyer, Johnson, Carragher, Ferdinand, Barry, Lampard, Gerrard, Hendrie (Mills 87), Heskey (Davies 77), Campbell (Cadamarteri 87).
Yugoslavia Under-21s: Kujevic, Dzodic, Dudic (Djokaj 58), Obradovic, Tanasijevic, Duljaj, Vukonanovic, Boskovic, Lazetic, Stankovic (Ivanovic 90), Kezman.

England 2 Ukraine 0
Friendly, Wembley, 31 May 2000

This was Steven Gerrard's full international debut. He was due to play against Argentina and then Brazil, but injuries delayed his first England appearance. Having his Liverpool teammate Robbie Fowler in the starting line-up helped to ease any pre-match nerves and Gerrard performed well, displaying maturity and assurance at the centre of England's midfield.

Goals from Fowler and Adams gave England a comfortable victory as national boss Kevin Keegan prepared his team for the European Championship finals due to be held later that summer. Ukraine did have one world-class talent in their line-up, AC Milan's brilliant striker Andriy Shevchenko, but even he could not get the better of Adams, Campbell and Southgate at the heart of England's defence.

Steven Gerrard had impressed all football observers on his England debut and was expected to be in Keegan's squad for Euro 2000. Injury, however, would limit his involvement in the tournament to just one substitute appearance against Germany. Steven Gerrard said after the Ukraine game, 'I did feel some nerves before the start but I asked Michael Owen about how he deals with it. He gave me a few tips.'

England: Martyn, Southgate, Adams, Campbell, Beckham, Gerrard (Dyer 81), Scholes (Barmby 73), Neville (Barry 73), McManaman, Fowler (Heskey 46), Shearer.
Ukraine: Kernozenko, Luzhny, Holovko, Popov, Vashuk, Dmitrulin, Kandaurov (Moroz 46), Tymoschuk, Husin, Shevchenko, Rebrov.

Liverpool 4 Arsenal 0
Premiership, Anfield, 23 December 2000

Steven Gerrard scored Liverpool's first goal in this 4-0 dem-
olition of Arsenal. Christmas couldn't get much better than
this for Reds supporters as their team displayed the type of
form that could see them challenging for the Premiership
in the new year. Steven Gerrard was outstanding as he came
out on top in his battle for midfield supremacy with one
of the two players he admired the most in the Premiership,
Patrick Vieira. The other was Roy Keane and he had outshone him a few days earlier in Liverpool's 1-0 victory at
Old Trafford.

Gerrard opened the scoring after eleven minutes with a
shot past Manninger from outside the box. Michael Owen
scored the second and Nick Barmby the third. Robbie
Fowler completed the rout when he came on near the
end to score from twelve yards after Barmby put him
through.

Liverpool boss Gerard Houllier said after the victory,
'This is a great Christmas present for all our fans.'

Liverpool: Westerveld, Babbel, Henchoz, Hyypia, Carragher,
Murphy (Smicer 60), Biscan, Gerrard (McAllister 76), Barmby,
Owen (Fowler 80), Heskey.
Arsenal: Manninger, Dixon, Keown, Luzhny (Pires 45), Silvinho,
Ljungberg (Wiltord 66), Grimandi, Vieira, Parlour, Henry,
Bergkamp (Kanu 72).

Tranmere Rovers 2 Liverpool 4
FA Cup quarter-final, Prenton Park, 11 March 2001

Liverpool took on their neighbours from across the River Mersey, Tranmere Rovers, in this FA Cup quarter-final encounter. Tranmere were managed by former Anfield favourite John Aldridge and were expected to give Liverpool a tough test. His team had knocked out Everton in the third round and were keen to emerge as Merseyside's cup kings.

Liverpool boss Gerard Houllier picked his strongest team. Goals from Owen and Murphy put Liverpool in the driving seat, but Yates pulled a goal back early in the second half to give Rovers hope. Steven Gerrard then stamped his mark on the game with a close-range header to put his team 3-1 up just minutes later.

There seemed to be no way back for Tranmere. Substitute Wayne Allison had other thoughts, however, and he latched on to a loose ball in the Liverpool penalty area to shoot past Westerveld to make the score 3-2. The Liverpool side were aware of Tranmere's reputation for defying the odds and were grateful to see Robbie Fowler keep his nerve after Gareth Roberts fouled McAllister to give away a penalty. Fowler calmly tucked the spot-kick away to put his team in the semi-finals of the FA Cup.

Tranmere Rovers: Achterberg, Yates, Allen, Jobson (Challinor 60), Roberts, Parkinson, Henry, Hinds, Koumas, Rideout (Allison 57), Barlow.
Liverpool: Westerveld, Wright, Babbel, Hyypia, Carragher, Murphy (Smicer 82), McAllister, Gerrard, Barmby (Biscan 66), Owen (Litmanen 86), Fowler.

Liverpool 5 CD Alaves 4
(after extra time)
UEFA Cup final, Dortmund, 16 May 2001

Over 20,000 Reds fans travelled to Germany for this UEFA Cup final against Alaves, a small Spanish club who had come a long way in a short period of time. Marcus Babbel gave Liverpool the lead after just four minutes and Michael Owen laid on the second for Steven Gerrard after seventeen minutes. Ivan Alonso pulled one back for Alaves, only for McAllister to restore Liverpool's two-goal cushion just before the interval.

Alaves looked down and out as they took the field for the second half. Two quick goals from Javi Moreno, however, turned the game on its head. Robbie Fowler, coming on as a substitute for Emile Heskey, restored Liverpool's lead with a brilliant goal after seventy-three minutes. The Spanish team refused to give up and Jordi Cruyff equalised with just a minute left on the clock. The 'golden goal' rule applied during extra time and when Delfi Geli glanced McAllister's free-kick into his own net the Reds had won their first European trophy since 1984.

Liverpool: Westerveld, Babbel, Henchoz (Smicer 56), Hyypia, Carragher, Gerrard, Hamann, McAllister, Murphy, Heskey (Fowler 64) Owen (Berger 79).
CD Alaves: Herrera, Contra, Eggen (Alonso 23), Karmona, Telloz, Geli, Tomic, Desio, Astudillo (Magno 45), Cruyff, Moreno (Pablo 64).

Germany 1 England 5
World Cup qualifier, Munich, 1 September 2001

Apart from the 1966 World Cup final, this victory was probably the greatest in England's history. Very few international teams go to Germany and come away with a win. Therefore, England's 5-1 victory must be considered exceptional. After six minutes Carsten Jancker put Germany into an early lead, but England soon hit back through Michael Owen, who went on to complete a hat-trick with further goals after forty-eight and sixty-six minutes. Steven Gerrard's goal came just before the half-time interval and was without doubt the crucial strike of the match. Rio Ferdinand headed a Beckham cross down to Gerrard, who blasted the ball past Kahn in the German goal. Going in at the interval 2-1 up gave Eriksson's team enormous confidence. England's rout of Germany was completed by Heskey, who shot past Kahn after being set up by Paul Scholes' pass. In England it was party time; for Germany, however, it was regarded as a day of national shame.

Germany: Kahn, Rehmer, Worns (Asamoah 46), Nowotny, Linke, Bohme, Hamann, Deisler, Ballack (Klose 67), Jancker, Neuville (Kehl 78).
England: Seaman, Neville, Ferdinand, Campbell, Cole, Beckham, Gerrard (Hargreaves 78), Scholes (Carragher 83), Barmby (McManaman 65), Owen, Heskey.

Everton 1 Liverpool 3
Premiership, Goodison Park, 15 September 2001

Steven Gerrard had dreamed about scoring for Liverpool against local rivals Everton since he was a kid in Huyton. His twelfth-minute equaliser against the Blues was therefore sweet indeed.

Kevin Campbell had opened the scoring for Everton after only five minutes, but Liverpool hit back seven minutes later when Gerrard latched onto a loose ball outside the box and smashed his shot past Paul Gerrard in the Blues' goal. Gerrard celebrated as though he had just scored the winner in a World Cup final, the goal meant that much to him. Michael Owen then put Liverpool in front from the penalty spot after twenty-nine minutes.

In the second half, John Arne Riise wrapped up the three points when he shot past Paul Gerrard after a scintillating solo run at the Everton defence. Playing on the right of midfield, Steven Gerrard had a fabulous game for Liverpool and was the Reds' Man of the Match in a great display by Houllier's boys.

Everton: Gerrard, Weir, Stubbs, Unsworth (Gascoigne 45), Watson, Alexandersson (Hibbert 75), Gravesen, Xavier (Radzinski 45), Naysmith, Ferguson, Campbell.
Liverpool: Dudek, Carragher, Hyypia, Henchoz, Vignal, Gerrard (Smicer 85), Murphy (McAllister 77), Hamann, Riise, Heskey, Owen.

Dynamo Kiev 1 Liverpool 2
Champions League, Kiev, 16 October 2001

Liverpool Football Club was in a state of crisis at the time of this crucial encounter. The manager, Gerard Houllier, was still in hospital recovering from major heart surgery after collapsing just three days earlier after a Premiership game against Leeds at Anfield. Phil Thompson was in charge of the team that flew to the Ukraine and implored his men to give their all for their stricken manager. 'With the gaffer in hospital, winning that match in Kiev meant even more to us,' said Steven Gerrard afterwards.

Liverpool took the lead through Danny Murphy, only for Kiev to draw level through Ghioane early in the second half. The Reds knew that their chances of qualifying for the last eight of the Champions League were likely to rest on a victory over Kiev. No British team had ever left there with a win under their belts, but Steven Gerrard's sixty-seventh-minute goal gave the Reds a famous victory.

Dynamo Kiev: Reva, Bodnar (Husin 56), Holovko, Vaschuk, Nesmachny, Cernat, Ghioane, Gavrancic, Melashchenko (Idahor 80), Belkevich, Khatskevich.
Liverpool: Dudek, Carragher, Henchoz, Hyypia, Riise, Barmby (Berger 62), Gerrard, McAllister, Murphy, Smicer (Redknapp 80), Heskey.

Manchester United 0 Liverpool 1
Premiership, Old Trafford, 22 January 2002

To win at Old Trafford is always a source of great jubilation for the Anfield faithful. This 2002 victory was particularly sweet as it reduced United's lead over Liverpool at the top of the Premiership to just two points. Arsenal went on to finish the season as champions with Liverpool in second spot, seven points behind.

After the victory, however, Reds fans dreamt that this might just be the year when the Premiership crown would find its way into the Anfield trophy cabinet for the first time. The stars of Liverpool's fighting display against United in this January 2002 encounter were the Liverpool midfield trio of Danny Murphy, Dietmar Hamann and Steven Gerrard. Murphy scored the only goal of the game with a fine lofted shot over Barthez after Gerrard had picked him out with a superbly taken free-kick. Pitting his skills against the midfielder that he admired the most in the Premiership, Roy Keane, Steven Gerrard had an outstanding game in a fine all-round team performance by Gerard Houllier's boys.

Manchester United: Barthez, Gary Neville, Blanc, Phil Neville, Silvestre, Scholes, Keane, Beckham (Solskjaer 87), Veron, Giggs, van Nistelrooy.
Liverpool: Dudek, Carragher, Henchoz, Hyypia, Wright, Murphy (Berger 87), Gerrard, Hamann, Riise, Owen (Anelka 78), Heskey.

Leeds United 0 Liverpool 4
Premiership, Elland Road, 3 February 2002

Liverpool ran riot in this Premiership fixture against David O'Leary's Leeds United team. Steven Gerrard had an outstanding game in the Liverpool midfield. Gerrard had suffered a slight dip in form earlier in the season, but Gerard Houllier kept faith with him and the midfielder's confidence returned.

A Rio Ferdinand own goal opened the scoring for Liverpool in the first half, but it was after the interval that the Reds really took control. Gerrard found Emile Heskey with a defence-splitting pass and the Liverpool striker shot past Martyn for goal number two. A couple of minutes later, Heskey scored Liverpool's third after some poor defensive work by the Leeds defence.

Michael Owen wrapped up the game for Liverpool with a headed goal in the final minute of the game. At this stage in the season Leeds were considered to be one of Liverpool's main challengers for a Champions League spot, but after this thrashing the Yorkshire side never really recovered their form for the rest of the campaign.

Leeds United: Martyn, Kelly, Matteo, Ferdinand, Harte, Kewell (Keane 75), Dacourt (Wilcox 58), Batty, Bowyer, Viduka, Fowler.
Liverpool: Dudek, Wright, Henchoz, Hyypia, Carragher, Murphy, Gerrard (McAllister 90), Hamann, Riise, Heskey, Owen.

Ipswich Town 0 Liverpool 6
Premiership, Portman Road, 9 February 2002

Liverpool netted eleven goals against Ipswich in two Premiership games during the 2001/02 season, the away fixture featuring a dazzling midfield display by Steven Gerrard. He totally ran the show and had some soccer pundits describing his performance as comparable to Paul Gascoigne at his best. Gerrard was a bundle of energy as he set up chance after chance for the Liverpool strike force.

Liverpool's first goal came from the unlikely source of defender Abel Xavier. The second came from a Gerrard long ball to Heskey who shot past Marshall in the Ipswich goal. Sami Hyypia then scored from a corner. Steven Gerrard then set up number four for Michael Owen with a firmly hit pass that Owen controlled before shooting past Marshall. Owen then scored the fifth with a firmly hit shot. Heskey completed the rout with a powerful drive past the Ipswich goalkeeper.

Ipswich Town: Marshall, Makin, McGreal, Venus, Hreidarsson, Wright (Stewart 38), Peralta, Holland, Clapham, Bent, Armstrong (Magilton 70).
Liverpool: Dudek (Arphexad 55), Xavier, Henchoz, Hyypia, Wright, Murphy, Gerrard (McAllister 80), Hamann, Riise (Anelka 72), Owen, Heskey.

Barcelona 0 Liverpool 0
Champions League group stage, Nou Camp, 13 March 2002

Liverpool's hard-fought draw against Barcelona at the Nou Camp in this 2002 game gave them a chance of progressing to the knock-out stages of the Champions League. Liverpool, in fact, had enough opportunities to have come away from Spain with a victory but failed to take the numerous chances that they carved out.

The Reds took the game to Barcelona from the start and Steven Gerrard himself had two gilt-edged opportunities to put Liverpool into the lead in the first half. Both chances were spurned by the Liverpool midfield ace but once again on the big stage Gerrard did not look out of place. Barcelona had the world-class talents of Patrick Kluivert, Rivaldo and Javier Saviola in their ranks but the Liverpool defence kept a tight grip on them. Phillipe Christenval did hit the bar for Barcelona in the second half, but Liverpool, in general, held on without too many alarming moments for a vital draw.

Steven Gerrard told the press after the game, 'We went at them from the first whistle and I think it gave them a bit of a shock. They didn't say nice things about us before the game and we used that to our advantage.'

Barcelona: Bonano, Puyol, Christenval, De Boer, Coco, Cocu, Luis Enrique (Gerard 76), Motta, Rivaldo, Saviola, (Giovanni 88), Kluivert.
Liverpool: Dudek, Carragher, Henchoz, Hyypia, Xavier, Riise, Hamann, Gerrard (Barmby 78), Murphy, Litmanen (Smicer 69), Heskey (Baros 72).

Liverpool 2 Roma 0
Champions League group stage, Anfield, 19 March 2002

One of the great European nights at Anfield saw Liverpool defeat the champions of Italy 2-0 in this 2002 Champions League game. Roma looked shell-shocked from the first whistle as Gerard Houllier's team tore into the Italian superstars with a wave of attacks.

Heskey, Smicer and Litmanen were employed as a three-man strikeforce and it was no surprise when the Roma defence cracked under the severe pressure it was under. Assunçao fouled Danny Murphy in the penalty area and Litmanen calmly converted the resulting spot-kick. Steven Gerrard then saw his fierce drive pushed away by Antonioli in the Roma goal.

In the second half Heskey clinched victory for the Reds with a headed goal from a Murphy cross. Steven Gerrard won the midfield battles with ease and made experienced internationals such as Francesco Totti, Samuel, Panucci and Assunçao look second best. Every Liverpool player played his part in a fantastic European evening at Anfield. 'I know Liverpool are a good team, but I've never seen them play like that before,' said a shell-shocked Roma boss, Fabio Capello, after the match.

Liverpool: Dudek, Carragher, Henchoz, Hyypia, Xavier, Riise, Gerrard, Murphy, Smicer (McAllister 90), Heskey, Litmanen (Biscan 87).
Roma: Antonioli, Lima, Aldair, Assunçao (Cassano 68), Totti, Emerson, Panucci, Tommasi, Samuel, Batistuta (Montella 45), Candela.

Liverpool 1 Bayer Leverkusen 0
Champions League quarter-final, Anfield, 3 April 2002

Liverpool gave themselves a great chance of reaching the semi-finals of the 2001/02 Champions League after this victory over Bayer Leverkusen in the first leg of the quarter-final at Anfield. The German team had the outstanding Michael Ballack playing in midfield for them but in general the German international failed to make an impression on the game.

Steven Gerrard was instructed by Gerard Houllier to keep a close eye on Leverkusen danger man Ze Roberto, who could deliver dangerous crosses from the wing. Gerrard's stifling of Ze Roberto was a major factor in Liverpool winning the game.

Although Liverpool failed to turn on the style in this game, the result was all that mattered and the Reds travelled to Germany confident that they could progress to the semi-finals. Hyypia's goal came on the stroke of half-time when he latched on to an Owen pass from a Riise corner to shoot home from two yards out.

Liverpool's dreams of a semi-final place ended in tatters when Bayer Leverkusen won the second leg 4-2 in Germany.

Liverpool: Dudek, Riise, Carragher, Henchoz, Hyypia, Hamann, Gerrard, Murphy, Smicer (Berger 75), Heskey, Owen (Litmanen 70).

Bayer Leverkusen: Butt, Ze Roberto, Placente, Basturk, Ballack, Lucio, Schneider, Sebesken, Ramelow, Neuville (Kirsten 72), Babatov (Zivkovic 65).

Sunderland 0 Liverpool 1
Premiership, Stadium of Light, 13 April 2002

Steven Gerrard had a great game in this Premiership encounter against Sunderland. Liverpool's 1-0 victory kept them in contention for the Premiership title and lifted the spirits at Anfield after their disastrous 4-2 defeat against Bayer Leverkusen just four days earlier in the Champions League semi-final.

The only goal of the game came after fifty-five minutes when Michael Owen ran on to Steven Gerrard's inch-perfect defence-splitting pass to calmly chip over Thomas Sorensen in the Sunderland goal. Sunderland came back at Liverpool but the Reds held on for a vital victory. Steven Gerrard ran the midfield and his display did his chances of being in England's 2002 World Cup party no harm at all.

This victory ensured that Liverpool would be playing in the following season's Champions League as they could now finish no lower than fourth in the Premiership. For the time being, however, they still had aspirations of catching Arsenal at the top of the league.

Sunderland: Sorensen, Williams, Craddock (Kyle 6), Bjorklund, McCartney, McAteer, McCann, Reyna, Kilbane, Phillips, Quinn.
Liverpool: Dudek, Carragher, Hyypia, Henchoz, Xavier, Riise, Hamann, Gerrard, Litmanen (Murphy 6), Owen, Anelka.

England 4 Paraguay 0
Friendly, Anfield, 17 April 2002

Steven Gerrard was one of the Liverpool players in the England team that took on Paraguay at Anfield in 2002. Michael Owen also started, while Danny Murphy and Jamie Carragher, as well as former Anfield favourite Robbie Fowler, came on in the second half. Gerrard, Carragher and Owen had been at Liverpool since they were youngsters and the icing on the cake was the fact that Owen was named as captain for the game.

Sven-Goran Eriksson had said that England needed a confidence booster before travelling to the Far East for the World Cup finals later that summer. England got off to a dream start when Steven Gerrard picked out Owen with a pinpoint cross to allow the Liverpool striker to head England into the lead after just three minutes. The Liverpool crowd went crazy as their homegrown heroes threatened to run riot. Gerrard and Owen combined to create numerous chances and their Anfield teammate Danny Murphy scored with a deflected shot just after the interval. Another deflected goal, this time from a Darius Vassell shot, and an own goal late in the game gave England a 4-0 victory.

England: Seaman, Gary Neville (Lampard 68), Keown (Mills 46), Southgate (Carragher 68), Bridge (Phil Neville 68), Gerrard (Sinclair 46), Butt (Hargreaves 46), Scholes (Murphy 46), Dyer (Joe Cole 46), Vassell (Sheringham 68), Owen (Fowler 46).
Paraguay: Taverelli, Arco, Ayaia, Camarra (Cesar Careres 80), Caniza, Struway, Gavilan (Sanabria 55), Paredes, Bonet (Moringo 80), Cardozo (Baez 46), Santa Cruz.

Liverpool 2 Manchester United 0
Worthington Cup final, Cardiff, 2 March 2003

Steven Gerrard once said, 'As a scouser, I shouldn't be saying this, but Roy Keane has been my favourite player for ten years.' This Worthington Cup final saw Gerrard go head to head with Roy Keane and prevail, scoring the opening goal. A second late on from Michael Owen ensured that Liverpool took the Worthington Cup back to Anfield.

On paper, Manchester United had the players to have won this final comfortably, but Houllier's team had made a habit of beating United and the Reds outsmarted Sir Alex Ferguson's team again here.

Steven Gerrard's goal came after thirty-nine minutes when his speculative blast at goal hit David Beckham's leg and deflected past Barthez to give the Reds the lead. Michael Owen clinched victory in the eighty-sixth minute when he latched onto a pass from Hamann and coolly clipped the ball past Barthez into the bottom corner. Gerard Houllier had won his second Worthington Cup in his managerial reign at Liverpool.

Liverpool: Dudek, Carragher, Henchoz, Hyypia, Riise, Diouff (Biscan 90), Gerrard, Hamann, Murphy, Heskey (Baros 61, Smicer 89), Owen.
Manchester United: Barthez, Gary Neville, Brown (Solskjaer 74), Ferdinand, Silvestre, Beckham, Keane, Veron, Giggs, Scholes, van Nistelrooy

Turkey 0 England 0
Euro 2004 qualifier, Istanbul, 11 October 2003

England needed a draw to clinch their place at the Euro 2004 finals in Portugal. The Turks had promised Eriksson's team a hot reception in Istanbul and they didn't disappoint. Steven Gerrard and the rest of the England side had been warned not to give in to provocation.

Gerrard began the game playing on the left side of midfield, but as the match progressed he played more as a left-winger. He won a penalty for England after thirty-seven minutes when he cut in from the left side and was brought down in the penalty area by Tugay. David Beckham failed with his spot-kick.

The game erupted as the two teams walked off for the half-time interval. Some reports claimed that as many as fifty people became embroiled in a brawl as the teams entered the tunnel that led to the dressing rooms. Order was restored and England held on for a vital draw after a tense second half.

England: James, Gary Neville, Ashley Cole, Campbell, Terry, Butt, Gerrard, Scholes (Lampard 89), Beckham, Rooney (Dyer 72), Heskey (Vassell 68).
Turkey: Rustu, Ibrahim, Bulent, Fatih, Alpay, Emre, Okan (Ilhan 68), Tugay, Sukur, Nihat, Sergen (Tuncay 61).

Sweden 1 England 0
Friendly, Gothenburg, 31 March 2004

This was Steven Gerrard's first appearance as captain of his country, but after a poor display by England it was not a happy outcome for the Liverpool midfielder. A goal from Zlatan Ibrahimovic in the fifty-fourth minute gave Sweden the lead in a scrappy game.

Sven-Goran Eriksson was using the match to try out Celtic's Alan Thompson and a host of other fringe players in the international arena. Gerrard's Liverpool teammates Jamie Carragher and Emile Heskey also made appearances for the national team. Steven Gerrard left the field after sixty minutes to be replaced by Chelsea's Joe Cole.

Sweden held on for a 1-0 victory after a game that failed to inspire much confidence in England's chances for the Euro 2004 finals. For Steven Gerrard, however, captaining his country was a dream come true. Liverpool boss Gerard Houllier said of Gerrard's captaincy, 'At just twenty-three his best years are ahead of him. This won't be the last time he leads his country.'

England: James, Phil Neville, Terry (Gardner 46), Woodgate (Southgate 46), Carragher, Hargreaves (Jenas 60), Butt (Parker 78), Gerrard (Joe Cole 60), Thompson (Heskey 60), Vassell (Defoe 12), Rooney (Smith 60).
Sweden: Isaksson (Kihistedt 46), Lucic, Mellberg, Mjallby (Linderoth 46), Edman, Nilsson, Svensson (Johnson 46), Andersson (Kailstrom 46), Wilhelmason, Ibrahimovic (Ostlund 90), Elmander (Hansson 46).

England 3 Switzerland 0
European Championships, Coimbra, 17 June 2004

Steven Gerrard scored England's third goal in this vital Euro 2004 encounter. A win was needed to give England a chance of qualifying for the quarter-finals.

Wayne Rooney scored two goals in this game. On twenty-three minutes the teenager scored his first after Steven Gerrard ran at the Swiss defence and passed to David Beckham. Beckham's pass picked out Michael Owen, who crossed for Rooney to head past the Switzerland goalkeeper with the minimum of fuss.

Rooney's second goal was more spectacular. Darius Vassell won possession of the ball and fed it to Rooney. The Everton youngster looked up and then blasted a fierce shot that beat Jorg Stiel only for it to rebound off a post, ricochet off the goalkeeper and then go over the line.

Steven Gerrard wrapped up the victory when Gary Neville sent in a cross that the Liverpool midfielder dispatched into the roof of the net. England's Euro 2004 campaign was up and running.

England: James, Gary Neville, Campbell, Terry, Ashley Cole, Beckham, Gerrard, Lampard, Scholes (Hargreaves 70), Owen (Vassell 72), Rooney (Dyer 83).
Switzerland: Stiel, Haas, Murat Yakin, Muller, Spycher, Huggel, Celestini (Cabanas 53), Wicky, Chapuisat (Gygax 45), Hakan Yakin (Vonlanthen 84), Frei.

AK Graz 0 Liverpool 2
Champions League qualifier, Graz, 10 August 2004

Steven Gerrard scored Liverpool's two goals in this fine 2–0 victory over the Austrian champions. All the talk before the match was about Michael Owen's impending transfer, with Real Madrid favourites to capture the Anfield hero. Owen was not named in the Liverpool line-up and looked ill at ease as he watched the game from the substitutes' bench.

The game was Rafael Benitez's first competitive match in charge at Anfield and a win was vital if Liverpool were going to reach the group stages of the Champions League. Steven Gerrard's first goal eased the nerves of the Liverpool contingent, striking a superb twenty-five-yard shot into the top corner of the Graz goal after a neat build-up between Kewell and Hamann. Gerrard's second goal after seventy-nine minutes made the game safe for the Reds.

Liverpool might have been on the brink of losing Michael Owen but the decision of Steven Gerrard to resist Chelsea's overtures in the summer meant that at least one great talent would hopefully remain at Anfield for many years to come. 'It's a good result; we need to be playing in the Champions League,' said Gerrard after the game.

AK Graz: Schranz, Standfest, Tokic, Ehmann, Pogatetz, Ramusch, Aufhauser (Sick 72), Muratovic, Amerhauser (Dolllinger 80), Kollman, Skoro (Bazina 62).
Liverpool: Dudek, Josemi, Carragher, Hyypia, Riise, Finnan (Potter 85), Gerrard (Warnock 80), Hamann, Kewell, Baros (Diao 73), Cissé.

Liverpool 3 Olympiakos 1
Champions League, Anfield, 8 December 2004

Olympiakos travelled to Anfield confident of progressing to the knockout stages of the Champions League. A draw would put them through and when the brilliant Brazilian Rivaldo scored direct from a free-kick in the first half the Reds looked down and out.

Also in Liverpool's group were Monaco and Deportivo. Monaco's 5-0 thrashing of the Spanish team meant that Liverpool had to beat Olympiakos by two clear goals to progress in the competition.

Rafael Benitez decided to introduce Florent Sinama-Pongolle and Neil Mellor into the action in the second half and the changes paid dividends. Sinama-Pongolle levelled the scores, then Mellor reacted quickly to a cross from the same player to put Liverpool 2-1 up. The Greeks then began to play for time, knowing that another Liverpool goal would put them out. The worst offender was Rivaldo, who annoyed the crowd no end with his play-acting antics.

Something special was needed to get the vital third goal, and when Neil Mellor set up Steven Gerrard outside the penalty area for a strike at goal, the Liverpool midfielder didn't disappoint. Gerrard's shot looked a goal from the second it left his boot. The Olympiakos goalkeeper could only grasp at thin air as the ball sailed past him into the net. Anfield erupted; the fans' hero Steven Gerrard had delivered again.

Rafael Benitez said after the game, 'Steve wants to win for this club always. This is one of the proudest moments of my career. We are now among the best sixteen teams in Europe; it's possible to fight for more things.' Liverpool had come mighty close to being knocked out of a competition that they were destined to win.

Stevie G's Golden Moments

Liverpool: Kirkland, Finnan (Josemi 85), Carragher, Hyypia, Traore (Sinama-Pongolle 46), Nunez, Alonso, Gerrard, Riise, Kewell, Baros (Mellor 78).
Olympiakos: Kikopolidis, Pantos, Anatolakis, Schurrer, Venetidis (Maric 84), Georgiadis (Rezic 75), Kafes, Stoltidis, Djordevio, Rivaldo, Giovanni.

Liverpool 1 Watford 0
Carling Cup semi-final, Anfield, 11 January 2005

Steven Gerrard's second-half goal put Liverpool on course for a place in the 2005 Carling Cup final. It was Milan Baros who set up Gerrard with a cross from the wing that Watford goalkeeper Paul Jones failed to catch. Gerrard latched on to the ball and side-footed it into the goal via a touch from Cox's head.

Liverpool boss Rafael Benitez put out his strongest team, a clear indication that he was determined to make his first season at the club a trophy-winning one.

Until Gerrard scored his goal Watford had looked the better team and should have been in front at half-time. Liverpool held on for a 1-0 victory and went on to reach the final of the Carling Cup, where they lost to Chelsea.

Liverpool: Dudek, Finnan, Carragher, Traore, Riise, Nunez, Hamann (Biscan 72), Gerrard, Garcia, Sinama-Pongolle (Warnock 78), Mellor (Baros 53).

Watford: Jones, Chambers, Cox, Demerit, Devlin, Gunnarsson, Mahon, Bouazza, Ardley (Blizzard 82), Darlington, Helguson.

Liverpool 1 Chelsea 0
Champions League semi-final, Anfield, 3 May 2005

Liverpool's victory over the new Premiership champions Chelsea took them to their first European Cup final since 1985.

Anfield was a red-hot cauldron of noise as the game kicked off. Jose Mourinho's team were experienced but it was doubtful that they had ever played in an atmosphere quite like this. Garcia scored a hotly disputed goal after just five minutes and, despite Chelsea's protests that the ball hadn't crossed the line, referee Lubos Michel allowed the goal to stand. Chelsea laid siege to the Liverpool goal for long periods of the game but couldn't make a breakthrough. Steven Gerrard played a captain's role in keeping the talented Chelsea team at bay. Jamie Carragher, Sami Hyypia and Didi Hamann were all outstanding as the Reds held out for a famous victory.

After the game Chelsea skipper John Terry remarked, 'If there was one player I had to pick out as my favourite player in world football outside Chelsea, it would be Steven Gerrard.'

Liverpool: Dudek, Finnan, Traore, Riise, Hyypia, Carragher, Hamann (Kewell 73), Gerrard, Biscan, Garcia (Nunez 84), Baros (Cissé 59).
Chelsea: Cech, Carvalho, Terry, Gallas, Tiago (Kezman 70), Makelele, Lampard, Geremi (Huth 76), Cole (Robben 70), Gudjohnsen, Drogba.

Liverpool 3 AC Milan 3
(Liverpool won on penalties after extra time)
Champions League final, Istanbul, 25 May 2005

Turkey's Olympic stadium was the scene of the greatest moment of Steven Gerrard's football career. Holding the Champions League trophy aloft for his beloved Liverpool was a childhood dream come true.

At half-time it looked like Liverpool's chief priority was to keep the score down to a respectable level. AC Milan had been sensational in the opening half. There was surely no way that the Reds could claw their way back into this game. A goal from Maldini and two from Crespo had put the Italians 3–0 up at the interval.

After a rousing team talk from Liverpool boss Rafael Benitez, the Reds came out fired up for the second half. Steven Gerrard gave Liverpool a lifeline with a headed goal after fifty-four minutes. Two more followed quickly, from Smicer and Garcia, and the greatest fightback in European Cup history had been achieved. Liverpool took the trophy after a penalty shoot-out. Steven Gerrard said after the game that there was no way that he could leave Anfield after a night like this, and he didn't.

Liverpool: Dudek, Finnan (Hamann 46), Carragher, Hyypia, Traore, Garcia, Gerrard, Alonso, Riise, Kewell (Smicer 23), Baros (Cissé 84).
AC Milan: Dida, Cafu, Stam, Nesta, Maldini, Pirlo, Seedorf (Serghino 84), Kaka, Gattuso (Rui Rosta 112), Crespo (Tomasson 85), Shevchenko.

Liverpool 3 Total Network Solutions 0
Champions League qualifier, Anfield, 13 July 2005

TNS, the team from Llansantffraid in mid-Wales, were Liverpool's first opponents as they defended their Champions League crown. The champions of Wales, named after a local computer software company, were made up primarily of hardworking part-time footballers who had failed to make the grade at a professional level. Goalkeeper Gerard Doherty was the TNS hero with a string of outstanding saves. Fernando Morientes in particular was denied by Doherty on a number of occasions.

The early TNS resistance was broken by Steven Gerrard when he scored two quick goals, the first a firmly struck shot past Doherty after fine Liverpool approach play. Gerrard's second came when he lobbed the TNS goalkeeper, who had advanced from his line. Steven Gerrard completed his hat-trick in the final minutes of the game with a left-foot drive past Doherty. TNS had put up a brave fight on a night to remember for the small Welsh club. Steven Gerrard also had cause to celebrate: it was his first Liverpool hat-trick.

Liverpool: Reina, Finnan, Carragher, Hyypia, Warnock (Zenden 64), Potter (Cissé 76), Gerrard, Alonso, Riise, Morientes, Le Tallec.
Total Network Solutions: Doherty, Baker, Jackson, Evans, King, Wood, Naylor, Holmes (Lawless 72), Ruscoe, Ward (Leah 82), Wilde (Beck 59).

Total Network Solutions 0 Liverpool 3
Champions League qualifier, Wrexham, 19 July 2005

Steven Gerrard took his Champions League goal tally to five for the new season with a double against TNS in this mid-July 2005 fixture.

Liverpool travelled to Wales already holding a 3–0 lead from the first leg. The champions of Wales played above themselves with TNS goalkeeper Gerard Doherty having a fine game. Steven Beck even managed to strike a Liverpool post in the second half as the Welsh minnows came forward in search of an equaliser after Cissé had put the European champions into the lead. The TNS goalkeeper, Doherty, kept his side in the match after saving a Dietmar Hamann penalty kick in the second period.

Steven Gerrard ended any chance of TNS springing a surprise when he came on as a second-half substitute for Alonso. Gerrard had his shooting boots on and scored two goals in the space of a minute to make the game safe for Liverpool. The Reds were safely through to the next qualifying game where they safely disposed of Lithuanian champions FBK Kaunas with the minimum of fuss.

Total Network Solutions: Doherty, Baker, Evans (Jackson 78), Holmes, King, Naylor, Hogan, Beck, Ruscoe, Wood (Lloyd-Williams 59), Toner (Ward 69).
Liverpool: Reina, Finnan, Carragher (Whitbread 54), Hyypia, Riise, Potter, Hamann, Alonso (Gerrard 67), Zenden, Cissé, Le Tallec (Garcia 59).

Liverpool 2 West Ham United 0
Premiership, Anfield, 29 October 2005

Liverpool went into this Premiership game against West Ham under intense pressure. They had won just 3 of their opening 9 Premiership fixtures and, despite the fact that Rafael Benitez had delivered the European Cup in his first season, in the league they looked a distinctly moderate outfit.

Club captain Steven Gerrard had demanded that his teammates began to display the fighting spirit that has made Liverpool a famous name throughout the world of football. Just four days before this game, Crystal Palace had dumped them out of the Carling Cup and the knives were definitely out for Benitez. Liverpool's 2-0 victory over West Ham was hardly a win that made the rest of football sit up and take notice, but it was definitely a turning point in Rafael Benitez's managerial career at Anfield.

After this win, Liverpool appeared to undergo a meta-morphosis and from being one of the dullest teams in the Premiership they became one of the most exciting almost overnight. The Reds went on a ten-game winning spree in the Premiership and Rafael Benitez began to be talked about by many of the Anfield faithful as the new Bill Shankly. The team began to play with belief and style again.

Liverpool's victory over West Ham, like their overnight transformation into an attractive outfit to watch, was inspired by Steven Gerrard's fabulous midfield perform-ance. The goals against West Ham were scored by Xabi Alonso and Bolo Zenden, the inspiration came courtesy of Steven Gerrard. This game proved to be a major turning point in Liverpool's season.

Liverpool: Reina, Finnan, Carragher, Hyypia, Riise, Gerrard, Sissoko, Alonso, Garcia, Cissé (Zenden 73), Morientes (Crouch 89).

West Ham United: Hislop, Repka (Collins 81), Ferdinand, Gabbidon, Konchesky, Bellion (Aliadière 60), Reo-Coker, Benayoun, Mullins, Etherington (Sheringham 67), Harewood.

Aston Villa 0 Liverpool 2
Premiership, Villa Park, 5 November 2005

Steven Gerrard's 300th game for Liverpool was this afternoon encounter against David O'Leary's under-achieving Aston Villa side. Rafael Benitez had said before the game that Steven Gerrard would play on the right side of midfield but after thirty minutes the Liverpool boss switched his captain to a more central role. After a relatively uneventful first half, the versatile Gerrard was then switched to the left of midfield before being allowed to adopt a more roaming role. England boss Sven-Goran Eriksson had said many times that what he particularly liked about Steven Gerrard was the fact that he could play anywhere and was outstanding in many positions for club and country. Once again, Gerrard was Liverpool's star player in an uninspiring Premiership game.

Aston Villa had former Reds favourite Milan Baros in their line-up. Baros had few opportunities to shine as the Liverpool defence kept a tight grip on the Villa forwards. Inevitably, it was Steven Gerrard who broke the deadlock when he converted a spot-kick after Ridgewell had brought down Crouch in the penalty area. Just four minutes later, Xabi Alonso made the game safe for Liverpool when he scored from close range.

It might not have been a classic, but Liverpool were happy to come away from Villa Park with the points. Steven Gerrard had maintained his good goalscoring form at the start of the 2005/06 campaign and his 300th game for the Reds ended in victory.

Aston Villa: Sorensen, Delaney, Mellberg, Ridgewell, Barry, Davis, McCann, Bakke (Hendrie 82), Milner, Phillips (Angel 60), Baros.
Liverpool: Reina, Finnan, Carragher, Hyypia, Riise, Gerrard, Sissoko, Alonso, Garcia (Zenden 58), Cissé (Kewell 76), Morientes (Crouch 68).

Argentina 2 England 3
Friendly, Geneva, 12 November 2005

There is no such thing as a friendly between England and Argentina and this fantastic game would have graced a World Cup final.

Argentina and England were among the favourites to win the World Cup in 2006 in Germany. Right from the opening minutes of this game, Argentina looked like they meant business and Paul Robinson in the England goal pulled off some fine saves to keep England in the game. Inspired by the brilliant Juan Roman Riquelmé in midfield, Argentina threatened to run England ragged in the first half and it was no surprise when Hernan Crespo opened the scoring for the South Americans after thirty-four minutes. England, however, could boast their own world-class performers and the brilliant Wayne Rooney put his team level just five minutes later.

Steven Gerrard began the game playing on the left of midfield and then moved to the middle in the second half. Gerrard looked outstanding in whatever role Sven-Goran Eriksson asked him to play, but in the second period he really came into his own. Walter Samuel put Argentina back into the lead after fifty-three minutes, but two late goals from Michael Owen in a breathtaking last five minutes gave England a sensational victory. It was Gerrard's inch-perfect cross from the right wing that set up Owen's dramatic winner.

Argentina looked like they had been mugged, England danced a jig of joy. Probably the greatest so-called friendly in living memory had been won by Eriksson's boys.

England: Robinson, Young (Crouch 82), Ferdinand, Terry, Bridge (Konchesky 46), King (Joe Cole 58), Beckham, Lampard, Gerrard, Owen, Rooney.
Argentina: Abbondanzieri, Zanetti, Ayala (Coloccini 75), Samuel, Sorin, Rodriguez (Gonzalez 85), Demichelis, Cambiasso, Riquelmé, Crespo (Saviola 71) Tevez (Cruz 81).

Liverpool 3 Deportiva Saprissa 0
World Club Championship, Yokohama, 15 December 2005

Liverpool failed in their bid to win the World Club Championship for the first time in their history when Brazilian team São Paulo recorded a hotly disputed victory over the Reds in the final.

Liverpool reached the final of the competition with a fine 3-0 victory against Costa Rican champions Deportiva Saprissa. Peter Crouch opened the scoring with a sweetly struck half-volley from a Cissé knockdown after just three minutes. Steven Gerrard told the press before the semi-final against the Costa Ricans, 'I've been a Liverpool fan all my life and watched the great captains of the past lifting trophies during the real glory years. I watched the videos over and over again when I was a kid. I want this team to add a new chapter to the club's history by winning this cup.'

Gerrard had a fantastic game against the Costa Ricans and scored Liverpool's second with a thunderbolt of a shot from twenty yards out. Crouch added a third as Liverpool coasted to a fine victory. Liverpool's unfortunate defeat in the final after outplaying São Paulo for most of the game denied Steven Gerrard his ambition of becoming the first Reds captain in history to lift the trophy.

Liverpool: Reina, Josemi, Carragher, Hyypia, Traore, Gerrard, Sissoko, Alonso, Riise, Cissé, Crouch.
Deportivo Saprissa: Porras, Bolanos, Cardero, Gonzalez, Drummond, Centeno, Gomez, Saborio, Badilla, Azofeifa, Bennett.

Liverpool 2 Newcastle United 0
Premiership, Anfield, 26 December 2005

Throughout the 2005/06 season, Steven Gerrard had looked to be the best midfielder in Britain. By Christmas Gerrard was deservedly being acclaimed as one of the best in Europe, if not the world.

His display against Newcastle on Boxing Day 2005 was nothing short of sensational. Gerrard inspired his team to put Graeme Souness's boys under the cosh right from the kick-off. Gerrard scored Liverpool's first after just thirteen minutes when he ran on to a Crouch pass, drifted past Stephen Taylor and blasted the ball past Shay Given.

Liverpool looked rampant and if it hadn't been for the brilliant Given in the Newcastle goal the game would have been over by half-time. Liverpool's second goal came just before the interval when a Crouch header was pushed onto the post by Given, but the ball was judged to have crossed the line before the Newcastle goalkeeper palmed the ball away. At this stage the jubilant Liverpool supporters began to bait former Anfield favourite Michael Owen with chants of 'Where were you in Istanbul?' followed by 'Michael, what's the score?'

Owen and his Newcastle teammates looked a distinctly unhappy bunch as Liverpool outclassed the Geordies in every aspect of the game. There had been talk before the game that Liverpool's failed attempt to win the World Club Championship may have caused Benitez's team to show signs of fatigue. Nothing could have been further from the truth as Liverpool romped to an emphatic victory. Lee Bowyer was sent off in the sixty-sixth minute for a foul on Alonso.

After the game, Steven Gerrard said that he was delighted with Liverpool's display, but not with the crowd's reaction to Michael Owen's first appearance at Anfield since his departure in 2004. Gerrard said, 'Michael should be a

178

legend here for all the goals he has scored for us in the past. He got a mixed reception. I don't think they were booing him much, but he should have got a standing ovation.'

Liverpool: Reina, Finnan (Josemi 78), Carragher, Hyypia, Riise, Garcia, Alonso, Gerrard, Kewell (Sinama-Pongolle 67), Morientes, Crouch (Cissé 72).
Newcastle United: Given, Ramage, Taylor (Bramble 28), Boumsong, Babayaro, Bowyer, Faye, N'Zogbia (Solano 45), Luque (Ameobi 86), Owen, Shearer.

Everton 1 Liverpool 3
Premiership, Goodison Park, 28 December 2005

Steven Gerrard said before this Merseyside derby that Liverpool were now ready to challenge the Premiership big boys Chelsea, Arsenal and Manchester United for the league title.

After taking his personal goals tally to 13 for the season against Newcastle on Boxing Day, the Liverpool midfielder scored his team's second goal in an emphatic 3-1 victory over Everton two days later. Gerrard was in majestic form against a poor Everton side who looked outclassed for most of the game. New Anfield hero Peter Crouch opened the scoring for Liverpool after latching onto a Gerrard header and Gerrard himself scored the second with a blistering twenty-five-yard drive. James Beattie got one back for Everton just before the break but a third from Cissé early in the second half made the game secure for Liverpool. Phil Neville and Mikel Arteta received red cards for Everton in the second half, but this was far from a violent encounter,

'We've got the bragging rights until the next derby,' said the delighted Liverpool skipper Steven Gerrard after the game. It was Liverpool's ninth consecutive Premiership victory, something that had not been achieved since the glory days of the 1980s when Kenny Dalglish was manager. Liverpool as a Premiership force were on the march again.

Everton: Martyn, Hibbert, Yobo, Weir, Valente, Neville, Arteta, Cahill, Davies (McFadden 57), Kilbane, Beattie.
Liverpool: Reina, Finnan, Carragher, Hyypia, Warnock, Gerrard (Garcia 85), Sissoko, Alonso, Kewell (Riise 80), Crouch (Morientes 77), Cissé.

Luton Town 3 Liverpool 5
FA Cup third round, Kenilworth Road, 7 January 2006

Steven Gerrard scored the type of goal that even the great Zinedine Zidane would have been proud of in this classic FA Cup encounter against Luton Town. Gerrard had been serving notice all season that he was about to take on the mantle of best European midfield player in the current game. His fantastic curling shot from outside the area that gave Liverpool the lead was nothing short of sensational.

Luton fought back and goals from Steve Howard and Steve Robinson gave them a deserved half-time lead. One of the biggest cup shocks of recent years looked to be on the cards when a Kevin Nicholls penalty in the fifty-third minute gave Luton a 3-1 lead. Benitez's team, however, are like the Liverpool sides of yesteryear and they refused to throw in the towel. Florent Sinama-Pongolle made it 3-2 and then a stunning strike from Alonso that dipped over the Luton goalkeeper Marlon Beresford before crashing into the net put them level. Sinama-Pongolle scored again and Liverpool's remarkable comeback was completed when Alonso scored from his own half, with Beresford stranded in the Liverpool half after coming up in an attempt to help his team snatch an equaliser in the dying seconds.

The Luton fans were distraught; their team had had the game won. When the dust has settled, however, they will probably reflect on the fact that they had just witnessed one of the greatest FA Cup ties of recent years.

Steven Gerrard was unhappy after the game about Liverpool's sloppy defending. 'It might have been a great game for the neutrals, but we are not happy with our performance,' he remarked. The crestfallen look on Gerrard's face revealed the fact that even after such a sensational victory, the Liverpool captain would probably have been happier with a solid 1-0 victory. Steven Gerrard is a great footballer and, if he wants it, will probably go on to become

181

an outstanding manager one day. His cool appraisal within seconds of such a pulsating cup tie, when interviewed by the BBC after the game, marked 7 January 2006 as the date when we probably witnessed the birth of Steven Gerrard the football manager.

Luton Town: Beresford, Foley, Coyne, Heikkinen (Barnett 74), Underwood, Edwards (Feeney 81), Nicholls, Robinson, Brkovic (Showunmi 82), Howard, Vine.
Liverpool: Carson, Finnan, Hyypia, Carragher, Riise, Kewell, Gerrard, Sissoko (Sinama-Pongolle 57), Alonso, Crouch (Kromkamp 79), Cissé (Warnock 89).

Birmingham City 0 Liverpool 7
FA Cup quarter-final, St Andrews, 22 March 2006

In a week that saw Steven Gerrard receive a red card in the Merseyside derby victory over Everton, the Liverpool captain was the Man of the Match in this fantastic FA Cup victory.

Liverpool went into the game knowing that the FA Cup was their only realistic chance of silverware in the 2005/06 season. Benfica had unexpectedly knocked them out of the European Cup and Chelsea looked like their second consecutive Premier League title was already in the bag. Victory over Birmingham at St Andrews was vital to keep the Reds' season alive.

Liverpool had a 5,000-strong contingent of travelling supporters to cheer them on as they took the field at St Andrews. Not one of them expected to witness Liverpool's record away victory in the FA Cup, but the Reds' 7-0 victory caused the Anfield record books to be rewritten.

Steven Gerrard set up the first goal after just fifty-five seconds when his free-kick was flicked on by Sissoko for Hyypia to score from six yards out. Gerrard was involved in the build-up for Liverpool's second when he centered for Peter Crouch to score. The third Liverpool goal came when Gerrard's long ball found Crouch and the Reds' striker exchanged passes with Luis Garcia before slipping the ball past Taylor.

Liverpool went in at the interval 3-0 up and were expected to ease up in the second half. Rafael Benitez had other plans, however, and told them to carry on in the same vein after the break.

Liverpool went goal crazy in the second half, scoring four more goals through Morientes, Riise, Cissé and a Tebily own goal. Birmingham's long-suffering supporters were stunned and vented their feelings against manager Steve Bruce, who had to leave the pitch flanked by a police escort.

For Liverpool fans it was a night to savour after one of the greatest FA Cup displays in the club's history. Rafael Benitez told the press after the game, 'I'm delighted with the result. Recently against Charlton we had thirty attempts at goal and couldn't score. Tonight, every time we shot at goal we scored. Sometimes you need a bit of luck.'

Birmingham City: Maik Taylor, Melchiot, Cunningham, Martin Taylor (Tebily 46), Painter, Pennant, Johnson (Bruce 75), Clemence, Clapham, Forsell, Dunn (Kilkenny 71).
Liverpool: Reina, Finnan, Carragher, Hyypia, Traore (Kewell 22), Alonso, Gerrard (Cissé 71), Sissoko, Riise, Crouch (Morientes 56), Garcia.

Liverpool 3 Aston Villa 1
Premiership, Anfield, 29 April 2006

Steven Gerrard was Liverpool's Man of the Match in this fine 3-1 victory against Aston Villa. Apart from scoring two well-taken goals, Gerrard ran the game from start to finish. His first goal came after sixty-one minutes when he made a long run into the box to get on the end of an Alonso cross to slip the ball home. His second was a Steven Gerrard trademark piledriver from twenty-five yards out, which left Sorensen in the Villa goal clutching at thin air as the ball hit the back of the net. Morientes scored the Reds' first, with Gareth Barry equalising for the Midlanders early in the second half. Gerrard's two-goal salvo came within a five-minute spell.

Steven Gerrard's goals took his tally for the season to 21, making him Liverpool's first midfield player to score more than 20 goals in a season since the great John Barnes back in 1989/90. It had been a glittering few weeks for Gerrard, with his side reaching the FA Cup final after beating Chelsea in the semi-finals. He had also been voted the Professional Footballers' Association Player of the Year the day after the Chelsea triumph. Shortly afterwards, just days after the end of the Premiership season, Gerrard had further cause to celebrate when his second child with partner Alex Curran was born on 9 May, another girl, who they named Lexie.

Liverpool manger Rafael Benitez paid his own personal tribute to Steven Gerrard as the Liverpool skipper prepared to join Sven-Goran Eriksson's England squad before the 2006 World Cup finals in Germany. Benitez said: 'Steven has always played with his heart but now he's also using more of his brain. He is one of the best players in England and maybe the world. After the World Cup perhaps he will be established as the best midfielder in the world.'

Liverpool: Reina, Kromkamp, Hyypia, Carragher, Traore, Cissé (Sissoko 65), Alonso, Gerrard, Riise (Warnock 74), Crouch (Fowler 62), Morientes.

Aston Villa: Sorenson, Hughes, Mellberg, Cahill, Bouma, Milner, Davis (Gardner 86), McCann, Barry (Phillips 82), Baros (Angel 45), Agbonlahor.

Steven Gerrard's England Record 2000-2005

Opposition	Home/Away	Result	Date
Ukraine (as sub)	Home	2-0	31 May 2000
Germany (as sub)	Neutral	1-0	17 June 2000
Finland	Home	2-1	24 March 2001
Mexico	Home	4-0	25 May 2001
Greece	Away	2-0	6 June 2001
Germany	Away	5-1	1 September 2001
Albania	Home	2-0	5 September 2001
Greece	Home	2-0	6 October 2001
Holland	Away	1-1	13 February 2002
Paraguay	Home	4-0	17 April 2002
Portugal	Home	1-1	7 September 2002
Slovakia	Away	2-1	12 October 2002
Macedonia	Home	2-2	16 October 2002
Liechtenstein	Away	2-0	29 March 2003
Turkey	Home	2-0	2 April 2003
South Africa	Away	2-1	22 May 2003
Serbia & Montenegro	Home	2-1	3 June 2003
Slovakia	Home	2-1	11 June 2003
Croatia	Home	3-1	20 August 2003
Liechtenstein	Home	2-0	10 September 2003
Turkey	Away	0-0	11 October 2003
Sweden (captain)	Away	0-1	31 March 2004
Japan	Home	1-1	1 June 2004

Iceland	Home	6–1	5 June 2004
France	Neutral	1–2	13 June 2004
Switzerland	Neutral	3–0	17 June 2004
Croatia	Neutral	4–2	21 June 2004
Portugal	Neutral	2–2	24 June 2004
Ukraine	Home	3–0	18 August 2004
Austria	Away	2–2	4 September 2004
Poland	Away	2–1	9 September 2004
Holland	Home	0–0	9 February 2005
Northern Ireland	Home	4–0	26 March 2005
Azerbaijan	Home	2–0	30 March 2005
Denmark	Away	1–4	17 August 2005
Wales	Away	1–0	3 September 2005
Northern Ireland	Away	0–1	7 September 2005
Austria	Home	1–0	8 October 2005
Argentina	Neutral	3–2	12 November 2005

Goalscoring Record

6 goals, against Germany, Macedonia, Serbia & Montenegro, Switzerland, Austria, Azerbaijan.

Bibliography

Jeff Anderson with Stephen Dove, *The Official Liverpool FC Illustrated History*, Carlton Books, 2004

John Terry, *My Winning Season*, Harper Sport, 2005

John Williams, *The Liverpool Way: Houllier, Anfield and the New Global Game*, Mainstream Publishing, 2003

John Williams, *Into the Red: Liverpool FC and the Changing Face of the English Game*, Mainstream Publishing, 2001

The Official England Euro 2004 Book, Carlton Books, 2004

Joe Lovejoy, *Sven: The Final Reckoning*, Collins Willow, 2004

Stephen F. Kelly, *Gerard Houllier: The Liverpool Revolution*, Virgin Books, 2003

The Liverpool Echo
The Liverpool Daily Post
The Football Echo
The Kop Magazine
The Liverpool FC Official Matchday Programme
The Daily Mirror

The Sunday Mirror
The Guardian
The Daily Star
The Times
The Sunday Express
The Daily Express
The Observer
The Independent
The Daily Telegraph

Other titles published by Tempus

Forever England: A History of the National Side
MARK SHAOUL & TONY WILLIAMSON

This insightful and fascinating account, which covers the careers of England's all-time great players and the team's successes, failures and near misses, is an essential read for anyone interested in the history of the three lions. From the amateur gentlemen of the 1870s to the stars of the early twenty-first century, with many wonderfully evocative illustrations, it is the definitive history of England's national football team.

0 7524 2939 6

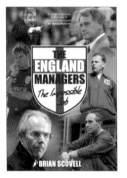

The England Managers: The Impossible Job
BRIAN SCOVELL

Since 1946 when Walter Winterbottom became the first England manager, the position has always attracted frenzied and critical headlines. Ramsey and Robson, arguably the most successful, weren't wanted, Don Revie deserted to Dubai, Graham Taylor had to go and Eriksson's departure was dramatically announced in the lead-up to the 2006 World Cup finals. This look back at the men in 'the impossible job' is laced with insights and behind-the-scenes anecdotes, making it a compelling read for all football fans.

0 7524 3748 8

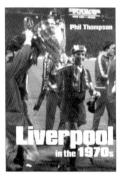

Liverpool in the 1970s
PHIL THOMPSON

When the legendary Liverpool manager Bill Shankly retired in 1974 he was leaving in place at Anfield the second outstanding team that he had assembled. With new boss Bob Paisley at the helm, trophy after trophy found its way to Anfield, the team achieving immortality with European Cup wins in 1977 and 1978, and by the end of the decade the Reds were firmly established as one of the great clubs in world football. This book documents, in words and pictures, the sensational exploits of Liverpool in the 1970s.

0 7524 3431 4

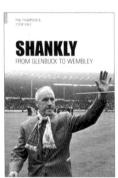

Shankly: From Glenbuck to Wembley
PHIL THOMPSON & STEVE HALE

Bill Shankly is the man who shaped Liverpool Football Club. His legendary status on Merseyside and within the history of the game cannot be overstated. Having been in charge at Carlisle, Grimsby, Workington and Huddersfield, he arrived at a struggling Liverpool in 1959 and transformed the club. This delightful illustrated biography records his life – from his birth in Glenbuck to the glory days when Shankly laid the foundations for Liverpool's rise to domination of the domestic and European football scene.

0 7524 2943 4

If you are interested in purchasing other books published by Tempus, or in case you have difficulty finding any Tempus books in your local bookshop, you can also place orders directly through our website

www.tempus-publishing.com